FL/

The Flashback series is sponsored by the
*European Ethnological Research Centre,*
c/o the Royal Museums of Scotland,
Chambers Street, Edinburgh EH1 1JF.

General Editor: Alexander Fenton

Other titles in the Flashback series include:

# A SCOTTISH COUNTRY DOCTOR 1818–1873

## ROBERT PAIRMAN OF BIGGAR

### Recalled by his son
### Thomas Wyld Pairman

*Edited by*
Evelyn Wright

TUCKWELL PRESS
*in association with*

The European Ethnological Research Centre

The National Museums of Scotland

First published in Great Britain in 2003 by
Tuckwell Press Ltd
The Mill House
Phantassie
East Linton
East Lothian EH40 3DG
Scotland

ISBN 1 86232 226 0

*British Library Cataloguing-in-Publication Data*

A catalogue record of this book is
available on request from the British Library

Typeset by Hewer Text Ltd, Edinburgh
Printed and bound by
Bell & Bain Ltd, Glasgow

# CONTENTS

# ILLUSTRATIONS

# INTRODUCTION

My mother's family, the Galbraiths, were merchants and ship brokers in the City of London, well documented in the London directories back to 1839. We knew they came originally from Scotland, but it took three years of research to trace them to the town of Biggar about 30 miles south-west of Edinburgh.

It was Brian Lambie, of the Biggar Museum Trust, who eventually put me in touch with my distant cousins the Millers of Edinburgh. Mrs Meiklejohn (née Miller) had done a great deal of research into the Galbraith family, and I shall always be grateful to her, and to Brian Lambie, for opening up a whole new area of interest and exploration.

We met Margaret Meiklejohn and her brother and sister, Richard and Sarah Miller, and it was Richard who handed me a bundle of papers saying 'Can you do anything with these? Some of them look quite interesting!' Among them was a yellowing, dusty manuscript, produced on a primitive typewriter in 1934, labelled 'The Pairman Family'.

The Pairmans are direct ancestors of the Millers, though not related to my own family. There are many links, however, and both families seem to have had a good scattering of medical men – in the case of the Galbraiths going right back to the late 1700s.

David Galbraith studied medicine in Edinburgh, and was examined at the Royal College of Surgeons in London on 24th June 1789. This was before the days of railways, so presumably he travelled by stage coach, or perhaps by sea from Leith. Unfortunately his medical career was a short one. His first job was as a ship's doctor on one of the slave ships, euphemistically known as the *Africa Trade*, and he died in Jamaica in 1792 at the age of 24.

Dr Robert Pairman, the subject of this book, also studied medicine at Edinburgh, as did two of his sons, Robert (who later married Sarah Galbraith's grand-daughter Jeannie 'Jessie' Watson), and Thomas, the writer of the memoirs. Both eventually emigrated to New Zealand.

Sadly both Margaret Meiklejohn and her sister Sarah Miller died in 1999, but their brother Richard still lives in Edinburgh, in the very same house in which he was born 87 years ago.

It is for his sake, and for all the Pairman family both here and in New Zealand, that I have edited these memoirs.

The original was a collection of incidents jotted down when the writer, then about 74 years of age, happened to remember them. It was necessary to select and re-arrange them, but I have tried to preserve their essential flavour.

It is hoped that this book will be of interest not only to the Pairmans, but also to the general reader, giving a glimpse into the way of life and, in particular, the practice of medicine nearly 200 years ago.

Evelyn Wright
Aspley Heath, Bedfordshire
2002

# I

# ROBERT PAIRMAN, FAMILY GROCER AND WINE MERCHANT

My grandfather, Robert Pairman, was born in 1784 at The Stane, which is now part of the farm of Heavyside about half a mile from Biggar on the Broughton road. He was referred to in the family as 'Robert Pairman the Third' or 'Robert Tertius', his own father and grandfather having also borne the same name.

He passed the early years of his life taking his share in the work on the family farm, but later moved to Biggar, where he became well known as the Family Grocer and Wine Merchant. His shop was next to the Elphinstone Arms Inn, encroaching on the street and looking out on the Auld Cross round which the inhabitants – mostly weavers – used to gather to discuss the civics and politics of their time.

I remember him as an old man spare in figure and somewhat bent in the back and knees. He cultivated whiskers and grew his hair somewhat long at the back and was endowed with a merry blue scintillating eye. He always wore, at Kirk or Mercat, what is now known as evening dress, that is to say a cut-away coat, vest and trousers all in black. A silk top hat, a gold fob with many seals and a silver-headed cane completed his ensemble.

On the knowe on which stood the Cross, a bonfire was lit on the last night of the year,

> To burn the auld year oot and croon
> The young ane on the Auld Corse Knowe.

The Auld Cross was regarded with great reverence by the people of Biggar. It is supposed and thoroughly credited in Biggar that the 'New Year's Day Fire' is a relic of pagan and Druidical times, and curative effects on man and animals were believed to accrue from rushing through the flames. I have seen a foundered horse made to cross a fringe of fire to the accompaniment of great shouting and jubilation.

Only once do I remember the kitchen fires being put out and re-lit in due time by a torch lit at the sacred flame and carried through the town by men and boys. Truly Biggar is an old community and strong in its traditions. My grandfather's house being so conveniently situated to observe the customs of the devotees of Baal, we children were sometimes asked to come and witness the weird and lurid sight from an upstairs window.

But Christmas was the great day for the gathering of the families under the patriarchal roof-tree. The Christmas party of 1864 is stereotyped on my brain, and I can recall many incidents that occurred on that particular occasion.

I was then between five and six years old and I have always had a most retentive memory. Uncle James from Peebles showed a number of tricks with hats and coins and handkerchiefs, bewildering and tiring to a young sensitive brain, and I was just beginning to yawn when he produced a little box and set it on the table: 'This is Aaron's serpent'; and lo and behold after he applied a match a veritable reptile reared its ugly head and went squirming and grovelling across the table to the terror of the remote descendants of Mother Eve.

Then we were taken into another room, where a real fairy tree stood in a corner, lit with innumerable small candles and bearing a heterogeneous variety of fruits. Did ever human eye behold such a tree? The influence of Prince Albert, the Queen's consort, was germanising at that time some of our insular customs, and the Christmas tree was then an innovation. I am certain it was the first ever seen in Biggar.

Some few miles out of Biggar at the back of the hill called

Corse Cryne, a locality of historical interest as being once the boundary between England and Scotland, lies the little Kirk of Kilbucho. It is now in ruins and these are the only remnants of an ancient village of the Culdees, but the massive mountains still remain, and the deep, dark valleys and the hill-whaups yet send forth their eerie cry to disturb the eternal silences.

Quite close to the picturesque ruins of the Kirk is the farm steading of **Mitchelhill**. Here at the beginning of the nineteenth century lived John Davidson, farmer, and Joan Grahame, his wife. There were a number of sons and daughters but the one most interesting to us is the daughter named Rachel for she was destined to be my grandmother.

After the shop shutters were up, Robert Tertius would hasten along the Hartree Road, pass Bogles-Knowe, and ascend the steep and winding Cross Cryne to the precincts of Mitchelhill, where he would awaken the echoes by a plaintive tootle on the flute, to the surprise of the wild curlew but to the understanding of his darling Rachel.

In due time they were married and Robert brought his wife home to Biggar. But do not imagine this operation was accomplished with any magnificence of pomp or circumstance. The vehicle employed was a good plain common Scotch cart. But stay a bit. When about half-way they descended, and made a detour on foot. This was a clever stratagem to delude a number of Biggar worthies who were waiting at the Town-foot to quiz and banter the newly married pair.

At the moment when the driver with his destitute cart reached the town, the couple were sitting in a bush on the roadside, where they remained till late in the afternoon and then wended their way by Pyet Knowe through the 'bogs' by the burnside, up the Loan, across the street and so home – undetected. This bush was still flourishing when I left Biggar on 21st March 1884.

My grandfather was a very methodical man, and so long as

strength permitted, took his morning's stroll down John's Loan to Biggar Burn, returning by the path leading past the North United Presbyterian (U.P.) Church Manse, where he would generally inquire after the minister. He was a man of confirmed religious convictions and early in life became associated with the Church and every other movement tending to the elevation and improvement of the community.

He was one of the originators of the Biggar Bible Association, which carried on its good work before the National Bible Society of Scotland was formed. This association was instituted on December 19th 1810, the Rev. Patrick Molleson of Walston being President and Robert Pairman, Biggar, Secretary. The latter would then be 26 years old. In a report written by my grandfather dated September 1st 1812 we find the following data. During the 18 months of its existence the receipts were £112 sterling and the subscription to the Association one penny a week. Of the receipts, £97 was handed to the Edinburgh Bible Society and the remainder expended in supplying local exigencies.

A number of the aged poor were provided with large typed Bibles 'which were uniformly received with gratitude which afforded the best assurance that they would be well employed'. Children who were orphans or whose parents were in destitute circumstances were also supplied. In the Autumn of 1811 the Association secured a number of Gaelic New Testaments for the use of the Highlanders 'who are accustomed to come into this neighbourhood as reapers'. It was found, however, that though a few applied, none of them were able to read their vernacular language.

On the arrival at Biggar of a number of French officers, prisoners-of-war on parole, the Association thought it right to commission a supply of New Testaments in French and other foreign languages to be sold at reduced prices to those who chose to apply for them. Eight New Testaments in French and one in Spanish were very soon given away. These were politely asked and gratefully received:

# Robert Pairman, Family Grocer and Wine Merchant

It is surely not unreasonable, as it is most pleasing to indulge the hope, that in some instances 'the quick and powerful word' will produce salutary effects, not merely cheering the languor of confinement, but effecting a radical lasting change of character; and that some of these unfortunate men may in after life look back to the land of their captivity as the land of their better birth – their birth to holiness and the hope of eternal life. Should this be the result of our labours in but one instance they will be abundantly rewarded. The happy consequences which may flow from such an event, especially in case of their returning home, are altogether incalculable.

These extracts give a good idea of the succinct phrasing and clear orderly diction of my grandfather. He devoted himself at that time to the study of French to enable him to converse with these **French prisoners**, some 300 in number (according to my Mother, whose own Mother married one of them). I have still in my possession a copy of 'The Dairyman's Daughter', in the French tongue 'La Fille du Laitier', and written on its cover these words: 'Robert Pairman, Merchant, Biggar' and 'Ayez la bonté de renvoyer ce livre aussitot que vous l'aurez lu'.

On Sunday afternoons my grandfather conducted a Bible class in his own house. I have seen some of his notes used on such occasions. These are written in a small precise hand, indicating a man of method, careful and analytical rather than discursive.

But it was chiefly as a Ruling Elder in the Church that he found his greatest enjoyment and the most congenial channel through which to exercise his social and religious proclivities. His love for this work was a sincere and engrossing possession. For over fifty years he never once missed attending a Sunday service in his 'ain Kirk' even though he had to come home from a holiday to do it. He had undertaken this work in the name of His Master and he would allow nothing to interfere with its consummation.

7

He was as careful over the financial side of the Church as he was over the devotional. On one occasion when service was being held the terrible cry 'Fire, Fire' was raised, to the general consternation of the congregation. A furious stampede was made for the door, but Robert Tertius was before them. The door opened outwardly. There at the back of the door, ajar little more than a chink, stood the Ruling Elder, calm, dignified, and unperturbed, with ladle in hand and held across the chink, insisting on the usual 'collection' before permitting egress and safety; a sort of Purgatorial Fire and payment minus the mass. Why should a holocaust interfere with the maintenance of the Kirk anyway? Why indeed?

In the year 1863 a number of his friends and admirers met and resolved, as a mark of their love and esteem, to present him with an easy-chair and footstool, both covered in rich morocco. The chair bore the following inscription, engraved on a silver plate:

> Presented to Mr. Robert Pairman, Senr.
> By a few friends belonging to the North U. P.
> Congregation, Biggar,
> in testimony of their respect for his character
> and their sense of his valuable services
> to the Congregation with which he has been
> connected for more than half a century.
> 1863.

His beloved wife Rachel Davidson died on 23rd January 1835 aged 49 years. The marriage was a very happy one. She was a patient and gentle soul, a devoted wife and mother and beloved by all. His second wife was Margaret Gladstone, née Gilchrist, a widow with one daughter Jane, who in due course married his own son Adam.

Now let me tell you one more story of my grandfather. On one occasion he had ordered, in the course of his business, a large barrel of treacle. This duly arrived and was at once tapped. The flow, however, was slow, sometimes even inter-mittent, so the top of the cask was battered in for thorough investigation. What was the horror and amazement of the bystanders to discover *in toto et in puris naturalibus* a Black Man! Oh Horatio! Horatio! there are more things in Heaven and Earth – and in Treacle Barrels – than are dreamt of in our philosophy!

In those days treacle was obtained from the plantations of Jamaica direct, but how the unfortunate fellow happened to find himself in a molasses cask was never discovered, nor, so far as I know, was any official investigation ever made.

This story my Mother told to one of her domestics, and anyone knowing the former can imagine how she would prolong its narration for the purpose of awakening intense interest and then suddenly spring the Black Man upon her audience as a frightful and unexpected dénouement. On this occasion the result was miscalculated. The servant remained stolid as a Chinaman, but at last a satisfactory shimmer was seen to pass over her countenance. 'What would you have done, Janet, had you been the first to discover the man in the barrel?' asked my Mother. The answer was of purpose aforethought, and decided as the rap of an auctioneer's hammer – 'I wud hae lickit him'! Chocolates were then unknown.

My grandfather died on 10th March 1867, aged 83 years. I was a boy of only eight then, and was not permitted to attend the funeral, but I remember the long cortège wending its way from the Corse Knowe to the silent city around the Auld Kirk, the shops shuttered as on a Sunday, all the house blinds lowered and the mourners with broad black crepe round their long hats and with white 'weepers' on their sleeves. In his own quaint words and spelling, Robert Pairman the Third had now entered 'the Pallace of the King'.

# 2

# ROBERT PAIRMAN THE FOURTH – THE EARLY YEARS

Robert Pairman the Fourth was my own father. He was the fourth child in the family of Robert Pairman and Rachel Davidson, and was born in that jutting-out house looking over to the Auld Corse on the Knowe already referred to, on the 22nd day of November, 1818. This was three years after the battle of Waterloo when George III was King, and one year before the birth of Queen Victoria of happy memory.

He was a little more than a year younger than his sister Agnes, familiarly called Nancy, and the two wee bairns became all in all to one another, each fanning the loving flame. Isabella Brown, the sister of **John Brown** of 'Rab' fame, once told me that she remembered my father when he was quite a little boy. She said that he was a bashful and thoughtful wee chap and of a retiring disposition, and when sent to the Manse to ask for the Minister would stand patiently watching the back door till someone came out, rather than knock and so bring himself unduly into notice. His sister Nancy was very similar in disposition.

Robert received the rudiments of his education at the Biggar Parish School then taught by a Mr. Richard Scott. Relics of this old School still exist. Coming from the Railway Station and after crossing the burn by the Neilson Bridge you may see, on the right-hand side of the street near the brow of the first rise, a cottage whose doorway is supported by two stone columns. These once adorned the interior of the Primitive Parish School, and a delinquent pupil was frequently made to embrace a pillar and have his wrists bound by a strap on the other side. Thus securely manacled and restrained, he could not effectively wriggle, and so was in a convenient and passive position for further centripetal chastisement. These pillars stood close to one another and a minor punishment was administered by making a pupil thrust his arm and hand between the two and in this position receive on his palm the tawse wielded by the master, who stood hidden on the other side. Waiting for the descent of this pliant sword of an up-to-date Damocles must have been as mentally painful as the physical castigation itself.

This Primitive School was built in 1798. Half of it was the schoolmaster's house, and the other half the school itself. Later the whole building was the Teacher's residence. One of the windows in the upper storey was always darkened, and the room itself was permanently locked up because a former teacher, Mr. Wilkie – or his wife – committed suicide therein. We boys sometimes saw a grinning face at this window and trembled, but the vision may have been subjective only, like Macbeth's classical dagger.

The school accommodation ultimately became too small and about 1830 an addition was made to it, thus dividing the school into the 'Big Room' and the 'Little Room'. Between these were the two pillars aforesaid. Here the Teacher stood when addressing the whole school or when leading the morning and afternoon devotions in which latter the pupils reverently repeated the Lord's Prayer.

In my time this closing prayer was yelled at the topmost pitch of our young and lusty voices but this was in another school (now the Municipal Council Chamber) erected in 1849 or thereabouts. The big room of the old School then became the kitchen of the Teacher's house, the wee room being demolished. The celebrated pillars at this time were removed to their present position to the great regret of many an old boy who had woven around them a garland of tender romance.

When my father was a pupil there were five classes named from the books employed in them, viz:- the Twopenny, the Fourpenny, the Tenpenny, the Testament, and the Bible. The School assembled on Saturday forenoons for general exercises and the revision of lessons learned during the week. The Teacher, Richard Scott, is described as 'a good classical scholar and a man of genial disposition and varied information but of somewhat indolent habits'.

I wonder what the boys considered a 'genial disposition' when they were tied to a pillar awaiting further developments. But certainly they carried away no malice, for many years afterwards they presented him with a testimonial, couched in appreciative terms, and freighted with a purse of sovereigns. At this meeting of old pupils my father, who was in the Chair, spoke in quite loving words of the auld dominie and these were homologated by all present. George Wilson, for many years a wright in Biggar, was a fellow pupil and he told me that 'Robert Pairman was the only laddie wi' brains amang us and the only callant that ever learnt his lessons'. This George Wilson was heavily pockmarked and was one of my father's first patients when he began practice in Biggar. Smallpox at that time was as common as measles but much more deadly and disfiguring.

In the year 1830 his school days at Biggar came to an end, and from a certificate granted on leaving we find that he was taught all the usual subjects current at that time and that the Science of Geometry held a prominent place.

**Robert Forsyth** (1766–1845) attended this same school a generation or so before. He was the only son of the bellman and gravedigger of Biggar and his mother's name was Marion Pairman, to whom my father claimed kin, but what the exact relationship was I cannot now tell.

This man of so humble parentage developed extraordinary literary and philosophic gifts. His mother may have been a sister of Robert Pairman the Second and consequently a grand-aunt of my father. Whether this be so or not, Forsyth was mounted on a mental pedestal as a model of perseverance and final achievement to encourage the less gifted and less ambitious generations who came after him.

My father's eldest brother, John, had given no signs above drab mediocrity at school and a story is still remembered about him. 'How did you get on at school to-day, Johnie?' asked his father. 'Oh, fine', said Johnie in a gay and self-satisfied manner. 'How do you know?' 'The Maister tellt me.' 'What did he say?' 'Johnie, ma man, ye're very defeecient.' So when Robert shewed a decided love of learning, his kind and affectionate father began to see visions and to dream dreams.

When he was twelve years of age, Robert was sent to a Classical Academy in Edinburgh conducted by a Mr. John Lawrie under whom he studied for two and a half years, attaining in Latin and Greek great proficiency. Before leaving this Academy he was presented with a Certificate of Merit and carried off a First Prize. The certificate states that 'his temper, manners, and behaviour were uniformly the most amiable and praiseworthy'. His industry in pursuit of knowledge was sincere, and he worked according to method. I remember seeing a plan drawn up by himself in which every day and every hour of the day had its allotted task. In fact his whole life seems to have been passed in 'redeeming the time'.

An incident is related of him at this period. His teacher had given him a Latin poem to translate and he found it an extremely difficult task but he worked manfully at it for many hours. Just as he was giving up in despair, Robert Johnstone of Biggar happened to call. This man, though self-educated, was a born genius with great linguistic and mathematical abilities, and to him the exasperated schoolboy eagerly appealed. Johnstone looked at the poem, quietly chuckled and said, 'Robert my man, this is a trick; the teacher has intentionally transposed the words and phrases in order to confuse you'. It was a paltry deception to play.

One of his exercises is still extant in the shape of an original Latin poem composed when fourteen years of age, entitled:

# A Scottish Country Doctor

### In Brevitatem Vitae

Heu quam plena malis, est quam cita: vita caduca
Ocius ex arcu tenso fugiente sagitta
Accelerat tempus, neque tentum quarvis habena;
Semper enim greesu celeri prohabitur annus.
Ut validum flumen, rapidum cursu, acribus undis
Volvitur in pelagus tumidum, torrentibus actis;
Sic hominum vitae spatium festinat in alis
Temporis, impatrius in terram reddere cunctos;
Namque vorax hustum non omnes demique vincet.

### On the Shortness of Life

Alas how full of evils, how fleeting is frail life
More quickly than the arrow flying from the
stretched bow
Time hurries on and is not restrained by any rein, for
Always with speedy step the year glides on.
Just as a mighty river raging in its course, with
Fierce waves rolls on to the swelling sea in full flood,
So the span of Men's life hastens on the wings
Of time, anxious to restore all to the earth, for the
Insatiable sepulchre will conquer us all at last!

At this time, Robert lived with his bachelor uncle, **John Pairman** the artist, whose highly aesthetic and literary faculties were surpassed only by his humanitarian and Christian characteristics. Uncle and nephew became fast friends. The former would entertain his charge with long engaging disquisitions on Art, Philosophy and Science, telling him of the vast visible glories of Creation and of the omnipotent Mind behind them.

These learned conversations stimulated the poetic and philosophic bias of Robert's dawning mind, and the effect was shewn in a magazine article composed by the latter, entitled 'The Study of Nature recommended'. Signing himself 'Ignotus', he, one dark night, with many nervous qualms, pushed the manuscript under the Editor's office door and spoke of the matter to no one. Doubtless he indulged in trembling dreams. The next issue was delivered as usual and Robert watched with anxious eye the face of his uncle as he perused it. He saw there indifference, interest, amazement, stupefaction and ecstasy.

The uncle then got up and paced the room in deep thought, gave his thigh a resounding slap and exclaimed: 'This is the most extraordinary thing I have ever experienced. Here is a fellow signing himself 'Ignotus' expressing his views on Nature exactly coinciding with my own and even making use of many of my illustrations. Robert, you must read it'.

This was a poser! 'I have read it, Uncle John.' Then a comic but delighted intelligence lit up the countenance of the fond and appreciative Uncle. 'Did you write it?' 'Ye-e-s' in a very meek and hesitating intonation. The next carrier's cart conveyed the magazine to Biggar with an effusive letter announcing that Robert had budded into a real live author. We can imagine the loving excitement in the old Biggar home. How Nancy would gleam and rejoice!

When Robert finished his classical education he, as usual, walked home to Biggar to spend his holidays. When a schoolboy at Biggar he generally spent these at Bogle Knowe where, in a little cottage embowered in greenery, lived a maiden aunt Margaret Davidson, who died in 1830, the year that Robert left for Edinburgh. Here he always enjoyed wandering about the hills, especially Culter Fell, the supposed cradle of his ancestry.

After his years of classical study it was pleasant to direct his mind to Botany, then a very crude and simple science consisting mainly of artificial classification. Natural relationships between species were not even dreamed of except by a very few, and 'evolution', which has now permeated every kind of human knowledge, was known merely as a vague speculation in the brains of some ancient Greek philosophers – known to students of the classics only to be scoffed at.

But yet he could not altogether suppress his interest in purely literary subjects, so with great avidity he turned to learn Hebrew in order that he might better understand the Bible. Besides, his long-cherished ambition was to enter the ministry. Before deciding this important question, he passed through a great mental struggle.

He was unfortunately afflicted with an inherited impediment in his speech which, however, only occasionally beset him. But on consultation with his parents and other kind and loyal friends he decided to enter the medical profession instead. But there was no remonstrance, no lamentation. 'If,' he said, 'I cannot enter the Church then I shall try to make myself the best doctor possible. Perhaps after all I may serve my Master as well in one profession as another.'

But before he began his medical studies, while he was still at Biggar, a visitor entered this peaceful home, one that had never been there before. For two years Nancy had been more or less ailing. Never at any time robust, she caught a kind of Influenza then prevailing, from the effects of which she never recovered. She died on July 20th, 1834, aged 17.

This was a severe blow to Robert and he felt the passing of his favourite sister very much. At the request of some absent members of the family he wrote 'A short Account of the Death of a Beloved Sister', a narrative couched in simple diction and shewing all the delightful partiality of a brother's hand.

In 1867 when my grandfather died there was a family conclave called to divide his goods and chattels. Robert was ill in bed and could not attend, but he sent a message to his brothers: 'Take what you like but be good enough to leave me the portrait of Nancy'. This was a little panel painted by the artist John Pairman.

Six months after this sad event, while Robert was absent at College, his beloved Mother also passed away. She was a sweet, kindly soul, the favourite of all and the pivot round whom the household moved. She was long remembered by the Biggar folk for her good deeds performed in a gentle and unassuming fashion.

At this time the Rev. Dr. John Brown, Minister of the Burgher Kirk, afterwards of Broughton Place, Edinburgh, commenced a Bible Class with which was connected a Literary and Debating Association. Here papers on Philosophic and Metaphysical questions as well as topics of a more religious character were read and discussed. This had the effect of fostering any dormant talent which the young men possessed, and to this Association many who afterwards rose to eminence in literature and the classics attributed their first inspiration, for example John Brown, Junr. Author of *Rab and His Friends*, **Professor Johnstone** of the United Free Church Theological Hall and his medical brother, Dr. Thomas Johnstone of Glasgow, the Rev J. B. Johnstone of the U.F Church at Govan and various others whose names have escaped me.

Robert, whose leanings had always been towards letters, contributed his quota, but the only paper extant is one entitled 'Indifference among Hearers of the Gospel'. In this address we see indications of the easy swing of a ready writer and the characteristic style to which he afterwards attained. The date of the paper is 1836. One of my father's published books, *Sceptical Doubts Examined*, had its germ in a philosophic essay presented to this Association.

But now he was impatient to mount another rung of the ladder. So, on the 1st day of November 1834 he matriculated at the University of Edinburgh as a medical student. He was then barely sixteen. His uncle John at this time painted his portrait in oils on a small panel and represented him holding a pen as indicative of his probable future. The portrait is very like him, and the hands, often a difficulty with artists, are particularly well done. Round his collar is an old-fashioned black stock, at that period quite *à la mode*, but to our eyes making him appear older than he really was.

In after years he occasionally spoke to his children of the

great luminaries who shone in the Scottish Capital when he commenced his studies.

**Thomas Chalmers**, that 'ruler of men', famous alike for his deep theology and unparalleled eloquence, was enrapturing his students by his words of wisdom and power in spite of his native Doric. He pronounced 'which' whutch!

**Sir William Hamilton**, the metaphysician, was emphasising in his own decided way that, in the words of an ancient philosopher,

> In the World there is nothing great but Man
> In Man there is nothing great but Mind.

**Monro Tertius**, the last anatomist of that name, is chiefly remembered from the fact that he was drawn into his classroom in an easy-chair. He was not so eminent as his predecessors, and his lectures were but poorly attended, partly on account of the unusual brilliance of his contemporaries in the Extra Academical School.

**Sir Robert Christison**, then in all the vigour and ardency of youth, was beginning to cast a glimmer of that fame which afterwards rose to influence the whole medical and scientific world.

Then there was that inimitable surgeon, **James Syme**, whose acute mind was looked upon almost as a species of divinity and who regulated his professional career by his own dictum 'Never believe what you are told but be always persuaded in your own mind'. Liston and Fergusson, his contemporaries, were distinguished in appearance but Syme was a very plain individual 'with a broad and somewhat expressionless face, with wonderful eyes, bull-necked, with neat hands and feet. He dressed in a black swallow-tailed coat, dark waistcoat and a large and showy necktie of blue and white or black and white check'.

His great weakness was love of controversy, and though very shy by nature, he entered the arena of disputation with relish. He and the great Simpson were continually at variance over professional matters. Syme was born in 1799 and died in 1870 and for thirty long years was undoubtedly the leader of the surgeons in Scotland.

He on one occasion came out to Biggar to consult with my father over a case of concussion in an aristocratic patient. The great surgeon was met at the station and driven rapidly to the mansion. He examined the unfortunate man, then turned briskly to my father and said decidedly, 'Isolation, Starvation, Purgation, Ice. When is the next train, Pairman?' Well may Dr. Brown say that Syme's spoken or written style was the 'perfection of terse clearness'. More of Syme later on.

But Syme was not the only great operator at that epoch. He had a keen and brilliant competitor in **Robert Liston**. At one time Liston was an anatomical lecturer and Syme was his demonstrator. But the two were in a constant state of squabble which ended in a sort of Corsican vendetta continuing for many years.

In 1823 Liston began lecturing on Surgery while Syme carried on the Anatomy by himself. Again the smouldering fire was blown into flame. Liston strongly favoured **Lizars** as a candidate for the Surgery Chair in the Royal College of Surgeons as against Syme, who also was an applicant, and Lizars got it. But Syme retaliated as usual and defeated Lizars for the Chair of Clinical Surgery.

Through Liston's constant irritability and alleged interference, he was debarred from entering the Royal Infirmary for several years, but ultimately his great eminence prevailed and in 1828 he was appointed Surgeon to this hospital. But the old quarrel broke out afresh which led Syme to open the famous **Minto House** as a hospital. It also led to Liston ultimately leaving for London (1835) to occupy the Chair of Surgery in King's College.

However, the real determining cause of his migration to the South was the appointment in 1834 of **Sir Charles Bell** to the chair of Systematic Surgery in the University, which Liston had hoped might possibly come his way.

Liston was the first in England to use an anaesthetic for a major operation. He employed ether and amputated the thigh of a man in 25 seconds. This created a great sensation in the Metropolis. Curiously enough, the great **Lord Lister**, then a student at University College Hospital, was present at this operation performed in record time.

Liston is described as 'a tall man, powerful in form, dressed in a dark bottle-green coat with velvet collar, double-breasted shawl vest, grey trousers and Wellington boots, the thumb of one hand stuck in the arm-hole of his vest'. But though cantankerous and truculent in appearance, and in reality in association with his fellows, he was a man of kindly and forgiving disposition and in the sickroom was 'gentle, sympathetic and encouraging'.

Several years after he left Edinburgh he wrote to Syme requesting a reconciliation, so they met at Syme's residence and renewed their friendship of former days, greatly to the satisfaction of both and to the gratification of the whole profession. Liston died from an aneurism soon after, and taking him all in all he was undoubtedly the greatest and most expert surgeon before the days of anaesthetics.

Another great surgeon might be mentioned who was a worthy rival of both Liston and Syme. This was **Sir William Fergusson**, elected Surgeon to the Infirmary in 1836. He too found his way to London where he rose to be President of the Royal College of Surgeons and Sergeant-Surgeon to Her Majesty Queen Victoria. He was a man of good presence and performed his operations 'with great celerity, boldness and coolness', quite necessary qualities in pre-anaesthetic days.

Sir William was demonstrator in Dr. Knox's anatomical rooms at the time of Burke and Hare's atrocities, of which more anon. In the year 1867 he wrote a kind letter to my father in which he says, 'I remember the occasion to which you refer very well, and have often been glad to learn that an old Edinburgh classman was doing so well'. I do not know what occasion is referred to.

Another great figure at that time, whose name is familiar in every country of the world, was **Sir James Young Simpson**, the discoverer of the anaesthetic properties of chloroform. In 1837–38 he was assistant to **Professor Thomson**, who was a lecturer in General Pathology in the College of Surgeons. He was chosen for this position because Thomson detected in him a man of quite unusual native talent. Simpson graduated in 1832, and became Professor of Midwifery in 1840, succeeding Hamilton.

In 1847 he first used chloroform as a general anaesthetic, and in 1859 recommended acupressure in the arrest of haemorrhage. The introduction of this method roused the ire of Syme to a white-hot fury. What right had a mere accoucheur to encroach on the scientific domain of pure Surgery! This led to a long, scathing and acrimonious controversy. One day Syme brought into his lecture-hall Simpson's brochure on Acupressure, read its title aloud in a sneering tone of voice, made a few contemptuous remarks, tore it in pieces and stamped them under his foot, the students meantime wildly cheering. There were decidedly giants in those days, and what is the use of giants anyway except to fight?

There was another eminent man of an altogether different character and profession who used to frequent John Pairman's studio, and with whom my father was quite familiar. This was the notable animal painter **James Howe**, the son of the Auld Kirk Minister of Skirling, near Biggar. One day a titled aristocrat knocked at his door and, on this being opened, said in a vulgar, impertinent and haughty tone of voice, 'Are you Howe the painter of Brutes?' 'I am', said the proud and imperious artist. 'Do you want your portrait painted?' Needless to say, there was 'nothing doing'. Poor Howe was like many another genius; he could make a fortune by his gifts but could spend it with more alacrity, and this he did several times.

But occasionally there were more gruesome tales to tell, and none more so than the story of Burke and Hare, later known as the 'Body Snatchers'.

# 3

# THE BODY SNATCHERS

On 28th January in the year 1829, an Irish labourer called William Burke was hanged in Edinburgh for murder. Let me remind you that my father left Biggar for the Metropolis in the following year. When the news spread over Scotland that Burke was executed, a sigh of relief and satisfaction went up from the inhabitants, especially from the young people. On this, however, hangs a tale, a gruesome tale forsooth.

**Dr. Robert Knox** was a lecturer on Anatomy in the Royal College of Surgeons and is considered by competent judges as having been the most brilliant exponent of his subject which the world has ever produced. He had a class of 700 students, and on account of the incapacity of his hall was obliged to lecture three times a day, and his luminous diction and accuracy of demonstration raised him in the estimation of his pupils to the height of a real hero whom they adored.

But one great obstacle to a thorough understanding of Human Anatomy was the scarcity of bodies for dissection, without which even illustrious lectures were comparatively vain. For the 700 students, not more than three or four were available in a whole winter's session. Most corpses were imported from Dublin and brought to Edinburgh by the Union Canal packed in hampers. Very few were obtained locally. They were received by Knox's assistant, Mr. (afterwards Sir) William Fergusson, the well-known London surgeon, no questions ever being asked.

About this time another Irish labourer who bore the name of William Hare started a common lodging house in the West Port Close. William Burke came to live in this lodging house in 1827 and found domiciled there a pensioner who, well-stricken in years, very soon died. Instead of having the body buried according to custom, the two Hibernians agreed to sell it to Dr. Knox, which they consequently did, and received due payment. The price paid for such commodities was from £8 to £14 a body.

This was easily earned money, and the diabolical idea of murder suggested itself to their minds in order to increase their earnings; with the aid of their wives this criminal method they proceeded to put into immediate practice. Their *modus operandi* was to entice travellers into their house, ply them with strong liquor and when sufficiently drunk lay them gently down on a straw mattress and smother them with another on top. This left no accusing mark of violence, nor was a sound heard during the process, thus completely deluding the neighbours.

In this cruel manner did they murder actually fifteen persons before being discovered by the Police. But at last Nemesis was near. At that time there lived an innocent, half-witted individual and kindly withal, named Daft Jamie, well known to the habitués of the West Port and its vicinity, and esteemed by them as a harmless, gentle 'Natural'. This poor soul was cajoled to enter the infernal lodging-house and never came out:

Lasciate ogni speranza voi ch'entrate.

He was missed from his usual haunts and suspicions were at last aroused. These were communicated to the authorities, but no direct proof was forthcoming, and justice waited. In the end the more execrable wretch, William Hare, turned King's evidence and thereafter found shelter in a nameless obscurity.

The populace exonerated Mr. Fergusson but deemed Dr. Knox as conniving with the murderers or at least as acting carelessly, though no corroboration of this surmise was ever discovered. However, it concluded the brilliant career of the illustrious anatomist. He disappeared from Scotland, but was recognised occasionally in London in a wretched condition, and the sympathy of many went out towards him. Before he was hounded from the Scottish Metropolis a turbulent mob, always an irresponsible monster, attacked his house, broke in his door, smashed his windows, demolished his furniture and many rare and precious objects of *vertu* and burnt his effigy on the street, Knox himself escaping with his life by a back window.

For many years after these events the children of Edinburgh were in a chronic state of terror and would run past the University gates, especially when the students or 'doctors' as they called them, were lounging about, for might they not seize, murder and dissect them? Their childish fancy declared that the students had always on hand an enormous kettle of boiling water to pour over their juvenile throats and then fix their mouths with sticking plaster.

But it was not only the children of Edinburgh who passed their young lives in fear and dismay. All over the Lowlands of Scotland the terrible threat of Burke and Hare kept youthful frolics within bounds and stilled the whingeing of dorty bairns. Don't I remember the appalling and intimidating stories told by the domestics round the kitchen fire o'winter nights, our eyes growing wider and wider and our breathing shorter and shorter? And every story ended with some horrifying allusion to Burke and Hare, said in a tense concentrated whisper, the young woman looking furtively over her shoulder as if expecting to see some devilish personality. Even rhyme was requisitioned to impress more strongly the plastic memory cells:

> Burke and Hare. . . . gaed up the Stair,
> And catched Daft Jamie. . . . by the hair,

About the year 1878 when a medical student, I was called one night to attend a maternity case in the West Port Close. The room was small with a low ceiling, and there I spent the night with the patient and two nurses. In the ceiling was apparently a closed trapdoor which aroused my curiosity. One of the nurses said to me, 'Ye're unco taen up wi' the ceilin', doctor. Dae ye ken whase hoose ye're in? Burke and Hare's. They had twa flats. In the room aboon they did the murderin and let the deid body doon through that hole, tae confoond the neebours'. I have never seen this trapdoor anywhere alluded to, nor have I ever heard of it from anyone else.

At the Churchyard gate at Biggar was a loupin-on stane for the convenience of corpulent squires and for ladies riding pillion or indeed one of their own palfreys. A little way within there long stood a small one-roomed stone structure with a window looking out on the pallid tombstones resembling ghosts when the moonbeams shone and scintillated. This was to accommodate the sentinels of the dead during the dark watches of the night when the so-called Resurrectionists or body-snatchers were prowling about like unholy ghouls.

Early in the nineteenth century this desecration of the tombs and theft of the recently buried bodies had become a flourishing trade, the anatomists, especially about London, eagerly buying them. Hence arose the custom of placing heavy gratings over graves, setting spring-guns here and there, and erecting watch towers. Many of the Biggar lieges were timorous and too chicken-hearted to act as night-watchmen but my grandfather Wyld had no such qualms, and so frequently had to mount guard with loaded gun, either by himself or with a single companion. Both loupin-on stane and watch-house have long been removed, but I remember them quite well.

Harking back to the purchase of bodies at Knox's Anatomical Rooms, I deem it right to state that **Sir Douglas Maclagan** has put these words on record: 'In reality Knox had probably no guilty knowledge, any more than his demonstrator William Fergusson had. The go-between was

David Paterson, the keeper of Knox's Museum'. This does not necessarily imply that the unfortunate David was cognisant of the real state of affairs. Sir Douglas also says the number of Knox's students was 'some 500'. Sir Henry Littlejohn is my authority for stating the number to be 700.

Before leaving this unsavoury subject, let me try to raise a smile, however wintry. One day a notice was hung up in Knox's room, 'Hamper. Opened 3 p.m.', which to the initiated meant that a body had arrived from Dublin and that a distribution of 'parts' would take place. This was always an exciting occasion, and the eager students with money in their hands crowded into the classroom. Scientific hunger made them impetuous. At last Knox appeared, opened his hamper, and pulled out – what do you think? Three veritable fat geese redolent of Michaelmas! Inquiries were made and way-bills examined. Everything was in order. The two packages were ticked off as having been paid for and delivered, but no trace of the missing hamper was ever discovered. It was surmised that the receiver thought it prudent to lie *perdu* rather than implicate himself in a legal process, and who can blame him? Probably he buried the hamper and its contents.

# 4

# MEDICAL SCHOOL

On the first day of November 1834 Robert Pairman Quartus matriculated as a medical student at the old University of Edinburgh and so began his Olympic ascent. During this first winter session he attended the classes of Anatomy and Chemistry under the last Monro and the distinguished **Professor Hope** respectively. He was thoroughly seized of both subjects, and during the ensuing vacation so far forgot his natural timidity as to entertain his old school-mates at Biggar with the wonders of Chemistry. They considered him a positive Thaumaturgus:

> And still they gazed and still the wonder grew,
> That one small head could carry all he knew.

But some at least of these boys remembered the experiments and their elucidation for many years afterwards, as I can personally testify.

On one occasion Robert and a fellow-student, eager to perfect themselves in Anatomy, remained in the dissecting-room after all the others had gone, when indeed the shades of evening were beginning to fall. They at last left together and some way along the street his companion exclaimed: 'I have left my book and must go back for it'. My father promised to wait, so he loitered about for a time but, getting weary, returned to inquire into his friend's delay. He found him outside the dissecting-room door almost unable to speak, with cold clammy hands and abundant sweat running down his face, in fact he was in a state of complete collapse.

## Medical School

It appeared that when the student entered the room it was almost dark and he had to grope his way. When doing so he happened to step on a spring connected with an articulated skeleton and the skeleton unexpectedly raised its arm and gave him a slap on the face! This was too much for human nerves, especially when horrible stories about body-snatchers and Burke and Hare were rampant, so he gave an agonised cry and bolted for the door. My father fetched the book for him and they resumed their journey home pensive and silent.

At this period there were three distinct Schools of Medicine and Surgery, viz: the University, the Royal College of Surgeons, and the Extra-Academical School. Dr. J. Smith, a former President of the Royal College of Surgeons, writes: 'To the joint fostering care of these (last mentioned) bodies we owe much of the advance of medical science and its teaching in our midst as well as the high value now set upon the diplomas emanating from their examining Board, and indeed the prestige of Edinburgh generally as a great Medical School . . .'

The diploma of the Royal College of Surgeons, like the degree of the University, was then a full medical and surgical qualification, and many great men – Syme among the rest – had no other. The extramural teaching was always excellent. Speaking of the teachers, he declares that 'there is a flavour of improbability in supposing that we can ever look upon their like again'.

After the first session there was a family council in his father's house regarding Robert's present position and prospects. Money was not too abundant and Robert promised to aid the finances by coaching pupils in the classics, which he eventually did. The result of this conference was that he left the University and joined up with the College of Surgeons. It was not altogether a question of finance for he was enticed also by the illustrious men then teaching at the various schools. In 1838 there were 225 practitioners in Edinburgh,

43 of whom were doctors of medicine and 182 surgeons. Let this fact speak for itself.

So in the winter session of 1835 he became a pupil of Lizars the anatomist and of his brother, the rising surgeon and worthy rival of Mr. Syme. He also joined Dr. Aitken's Class of Materia Medica and the Institutes of Medicine. I am sorry that I have not the data to enable me to enumerate and to comment on the various classes which he attended during his medical course of four years but it is well-known that in all the classes he took a very high place. Being a sort of freelance among the Halls of Learning, he was enabled to choose the lectures of whatever teacher attracted him and from whom he considered he would obtain the greatest benefit.

At the close of the 1838 session he carried off some very conspicuous prizes, including one of the two medals awarded by Professor Lizars to the two most distinguished students in his class of Surgery. These medals were of gold and silver respectively, and he obtained the silver one. It might have been a gold one but for a single mistake. I have heard my father say that there was only one student of whom he was really afraid.

On the day of examination – a written one – both competitors were present ready for the fray and the trial began. But the moment my father had handed in his paper he realised that he had suffered a lapse and had put 'right' for 'left' in one of his answers. He intimated as much to the examiner, but the die was cast. The other competitor got the gold medal and Robert Pairman the silver.

However, he was more fortunate in his other attempts and won the highest prize in the class of Dr. George A. Borthwick, lecturer on Clinical Medicine at the Royal Infirmary, as well as the first prize in the Materia Medica class of nearly 200 students conducted conjointly by **Dr. J. Argyle Robertson** and Dr. W. Seller, lecturers at the Argyle Square School of Medicine. There were other minor prizes obtained, one of which was a book called *Stokes on the Chest*, but for what I cannot now remember.

At last his great crowning day came and he passed his qualifying examination at the Royal College of Surgeons in the year 1838 when he was only 19 years of age, too young to obtain his diploma for which he had to wait several months. These months he spent in the dissecting-room, thus following the advice of Sir Charles Bell, 'Above all, improve yourself in Anatomy'.

Several professors at this time approached him and earnestly counselled him to give up all idea of a country practice, but to aim at a professional chair or in any case to practise in a city with a congenial atmosphere of Learning and Culture. Undoubtedly he was the most prominent student among the new licentiates and would have made a success in a large town, but there were other things to consider.

In those far-off days there was, in order to obtain a degree or diploma, a single oral examination only. There was nothing written. The aspirant was seated at a small table and had to face a semicircle of scholarly men, each a specialist in his own line, and to submit to a bombardment of questions from the right, left and in front, on subjects from Arithmetic and History to Medicine and Surgery, taking in by the way Geometry, Mathematics and Latin. Could a Spanish Inquisition be more grievous and distressing? It must have been a terrific strain on the candidate, but some at least, including Robert, maintained that they rather enjoyed it!

In this year, 1838, there were about a hundred new licentiates of whom Robert Pairman of Biggar was one. When he came out of the College after this gruelling, a number of students were awaiting him. Amongst these was Paterson of Carnwath, who obtained his diploma in the same year.

Some long years later, both now prematurely grey with the toils of practice, they happened to meet in consultation. Carnwath was always considered quite out of the world, the people were poor, the district mostly moor and scrubby heather, the distances extended and tedious. What could be more desolate than the dreary Lang Whang? My father, overcome by the barren, comfortless waste, exclaimed, 'Dear, me, Paterson, how do you manage to exist in a place like this?' Looking the very picture of despair and in a most resigned and prolonged lugubrious monotone he answered, 'Oh, it's juist an en-door-ance'. My father, always ready to see the comic side, laughed heartily, joined ultimately by Paterson himself.

Now that he was free of the inquisitors he sent a letter post-haste to Biggar, commencing in large schoolboy calligraphy –

I AM NOW A SURGEON! ! !

which of course was extremely gratifying to his Father and friends. But alas there was no proud Mother or clinging Nancy to participate in the rejoicing.

Soon after, he followed his letter home. Those were the days before railways and other means of rapid transport, but instead of walking as usual he, accompanied by a farmer friend, John Gairns of Kirklawhill, accomplished the journey on horseback. En route they called at 'The Callands' where resided a maiden fair who ultimately became Mrs Gairns.

# 5

# THE YOUNG SURGEON

The year 1838 was one of incessant cold bitter rain, so we can imagine the kind of ride the young surgeon and his farmer friend experienced. There was no harvest garnered that year, but the corn was pulled up by the roots to save for fodder. An old shepherd of Tweedsmuir solemnly declared that 'Ane couldna look for onything else than fludes as the heevans were gettin' auld and rotten noo and couldna haud it in', a truly calamitous condition but not unknown in other realms of senility!

It had long been the dream of his parents that Robert should settle down in Biggar as a country doctor and the subject was often talked about. In these things as in others it would seem as if some Divinity was shaping our ends and that we were being pushed into positions not altogether determined by our own will. Robert saw the finger of Providence pointing the way and he accepted it dutifully and humbly. After all it was his father's desire and he might go further and fare worse.

Biggar was the centre of a wide agricultural district with a number of villages scattered around. There was a good sprinkling of the nobility and gentry in the neighbourhood, the farmers were considered fairly well off, there were weekly markets which brought the country people into Biggar, and very large fairs were frequently held, bringing with them a breeze from the outside world.

The life of a Scottish country surgeon was then one of great hardship and self-sacrifice – more especially in the Biggar district – in fact it was the life of a slave with an oppressive and exacting task-master, to wit the conscientious call to duty. No railway, no telegraph, no telephone, no motor car, not even a bicycle, no aeroplane, no brass plate with 'Hours of Consultation'. On the contrary, the surgeon might be consulted at any hour of the day or night, which meant a continual physical and mental strain, with meals hurried and irregular, if indeed he partook of any at all beyond a mere snack.

Speaking on this subject, Robert himself says: 'He has toiled on a live-long day, through summer's heat or winter's cold, comes home utterly exhausted and stretches himself down in bed in hopes of enjoying a little calm repose. Alas! just at the very moment when he begins to think, well, all is snug and comfortable now, a loud knock at his door dispels the illusion and from an urgent messenger, who demands of the doctor that he must rise and ride, he learns with con-sternation that an inconsiderate herd's wife, far away among the hills, has contrived to exhibit symptoms of great distress even at that unseasonable hour'.

Biggar itself at that time was little advanced beyond the primitive village community type. The occupation of the inhabitants was mostly handloom weaving, the looms being hired out usually by George Cuthbertson of the Westrow, my great-grandfather on the mother's side, the 'webs' or 'wabs' being obtained from the same source. He was known as a 'Manufacturer's Agent', generally contracted into Agent and pronounced 'Awe-gent'.

The houses as a rule were of one storey with small windows and thatched roofs, very cosy in winter and cool in summer. The town is described as being 'in a very dirty and unhealthy condition with dunghills, peat stacks, noxious gutters and fulzie of different sorts seen in all directions'. But when I was a boy, born in 1859, none of these disfigure-ments existed, and the town was a model of cleanliness and salubrity.

There were seven other medical men resident in Biggar

when my father began practice. One was old Dr. Anthony Wilson, an Englishman, who, many maintained, was innocent of a diploma but he had the reputation of being 'unco guid wi' the weemen and bairns'. He lived in the Camb Cottage on the Culter Road across the burn. William Hunter describes him as 'a very amiable man and a cautious medical practitioner'. Cautious he was certainly, for he prescribed only and always 'Just a little cream of Tartar'. Dr. Wilson kept a horse and a donkey. When he was in a hurry to reach a distant case, he mounted his 'cuddy' as being the better and more expeditious animal.

Dr. James Summers was another practitioner with a good reputation and a very wide practice. He was also quite an expert in agriculture and the farmers often appealed to him in difficult and pressing exigencies. He died in 1864 in the Camb Cottage, his last words being 'In ten minutes I will be either in Heaven or Hell', and so it was.

**Dr. George Kello**, bearing a very old Upper Ward name, and in the days to come his two sons, Alexander and John, lived in a cottage with one foot in Biggar Burn, just across the Cadger's Brig, and were long contemporaries of my father.

There was also a Dr. X who held himself pretty well aloof from his learned confrères, in fact even from the general public, but who was a *persona grata* with the aristocrats. He drove about in the style of a grand seigneur. But even grands seigneurs must pay the debt of Nature and the day arrived when Dr. X had to bid farewell to all the pomps and pageantries of this passing scene.

There was an immense flutter in the purlieu of the grandees. Meetings were held to determine their plan of action. It was agreed that one of their own rank should be invited from Edinburgh to settle amongst them.

The blue blood was disconsolate and fermenting, indeed it nearly bubbled over when one gentleman remarked in a tentative sort or way that for a number of years he had heard excellent accounts of Dr. Pairman. What! The son of a grocer to touch their immaculate bodies! It was unthinkable.

But the allusion caused at least a rift in the lute and much irrelevant discussion wherein floated a copious store of pride, vainglory and hypocrisy. They finally resolved to employ the grocer's son till they could get somebody more suitable.

It is significant that when they did employ him they never left him, discovering to their confusion that even a grocer's son can be dignified and yet penniless, erudite and yet humble, a scion of the people and yet Nature's veritable gentleman.

But let us turn back a few years for we have not yet seen our hero launched into practice.

When this was at last accomplished on August 1st, 1838, he issued a circular bearing copies of some of his testimonials and distributed this among the people. He introduces himself in the following terms:

Biggar, Aug. 1838.

Mr. Robert Pairman, Jun. (Licentiate of the Royal College of Surgeons, Edinburgh) respectfully acquaints his friends and the Public in Biggar and Surrounding Districts that he has just commenced Practice here as Surgeon, and hopes he may so fulfil the duties of his Profession as to merit a share of Public patronage.

He feels much honoured in being able to refer to the annexed Testimonials from Professor Lizars, Drs. Alexander Jardine Lizars, G. A. Borthwick and W. Seller of Edinburgh.

In these modern days of 'professional etiquette' surely run riot, such an announcement may appear indicative of quackery, sordid and empiric. But at that time such declarations were quite customary and not considered derogatory to one's status in the community.

And now we can picture him 19 years of age, spare, pale-faced, with a studious cast of countenance, mounted on a tricky little grey pony with showy action, which he called Spark, riding about sedate and contemplative, but cracking jokes with all and sundry.

Success was slow in coming, with seven experienced, well-established practitioners in opposition, and the people themselves, though liberal in their politics, were extremely conservative where their doctor or minister was concerned. Speaking of those days, he once told us that in tyro innocence he made out a list of people whom he thought most likely would employ him, some on account of personal friendship, intimacy with the family or for some other apparently potent reason, but these were the very people who at first stood aloof. But so it is always!

It is interesting to note his receipts and expenses for the first few years. The receipts for the first five months are a little uncertain. But let us begin with January 1839. During this year his takings were:

| 1839 | – | £40:12:0 |
| 1840 | – | £85: 8:3 |
| 1841 | – | £98: 6:0 |
| 1842 | – | £125:10:5 |
| 1843 | – | £127: 1:2 |
| 1844 | – | £127: 6:4 |

Never at any time during the whole course of his practice did his income ever exceed £500 or a little more. Generally speaking, it averaged something like £350, but during his latter years he kept no proper account books. Some of the early entries are notable as throwing light on the conditions of practice at that time. 'Bleeding 1s 0d' occurs very often, and so does 'Odontalgia 1s 0d; Lancing an abscess 1s 0d; Midwifery 10/6, 8/6 and 7/6'. For extracting teeth he used the 'key' with its inflexible retentive claw, and did not favour the modern forceps.

The expenditure column is whimsically touching: 'Expenses of Edinburgh Jaunt 4/-; Carriage of Books per coach 6d; Jaunt to Lanark 8d; Edinburgh Jaunt 8/-; Donation to Biggar Scientific Institute 2/6; Seat in Church 6/6; Printing Circulars £1 11s 0d' and so on. The reader can infer from these items that the fees were preposterously small when compared with those of the present time, even allowing for changed conditions, and the expenses tell surely of extreme thrift and careful, economical management. *Tempora mutantur et nos mutamur in illis.* Quite so, but which is the happier? Then or now?

Country surgeons used almost invariably to dispense their own prescriptions and to keep what is known in England as an 'open surgery' and in Scotland as a 'doctor's shop'. My father followed this custom from the first and his original emporium was in the old family home. This arrangement suited all right so long as he was living with his father, but the time was not far distant before he rented a house for himself and convenient stabling for Spark.

In another paper I described a house built for Thomas Wyld in 1793. Adjoining this structure was the dwelling-house and shop of John Gladstone, watchmaker and portioner (1772–1851) whom my Mother called 'Uncle Gledstane'. He removed to another stand and the young surgeon was not slow in negotiating for the lease of the vacated dwelling, while Adam Wyld's old stable in the quadrangle through the close was retained for Spark. The shop of the jeweller became the laboratory of the surgeon.

For fourteen years the family lived here, in fact till my brother John was born in 1853; then they 'flitted' into a more convenient residence next the Relief Kirk (now replaced by the Gillespie Church). This house was built on purpose for my father and occupied a prominent position in the street and, though inconvenient in some ways, proved suitable enough for a country doctor.

Two incidents occurred in Gladstone's house which may be noted. One night the doctor was visiting a patient and the front door was left unlocked. Johnie the Baby and his Mother were sitting alone in a back room when she heard the front door open and somebody slither along the passage. Thinking it was her husband she called out 'lock the door', but meanwhile the sitting-room door was thrown violently open and a demented man entered, made for the 'aumrie' and cut himself a hunk of bread and cheese and quietly walked out again. Not a word was spoken on either side but this discomposing experience made an absolute finish to unlocked front doors.

Another night the household was awakened by the clatter of the front-door knocker which continued in a peculiarly irregular and erratic manner, most alarming. My father got out of bed to investigate, and on opening the door found only a horse without bridle or saddle and riderless.

He recognised the horse as belonging to Dolphinton Parish, an animal owned by the Auld Kirk Minister and which the parishioners, without the Minister's knowledge, commandeered when a doctor was wanted from Biggar. This was fairly often and the sapient quadruped, thinking no doubt it was about time for another midnight journey to the accustomed house, negotiated the paling, arrived at its destination and lifted the knocker as it had often seen its rider do before.

When the door opened and the doctor appeared and spoke a few words it was perfectly satisfied that everything was according to natural law and decorum, so it calmly turned round again and trotted virtuously home. Surely this animal possessed a glimmering of the Syllogism.

# 6

# FAMILY LIFE

In these notes, written at odd times as memory condescended to reach my consciousness, I appear to have an unfortunate habit of placing the cart before the horse, of fulfilling the prophecy before anointing the prophet.

I have already alluded to the birth of Baby John without first of all introducing the necessary Mother.

In the year 1846 the practice was considered a fairly good one and it was rapidly increasing. My father, in spite of the paltry fees, was putting away from time to time a little money.

For instance he had a few shares in the Biggar Gas Company and he had bought five £20 shares in the Ayrshire Iron Company, and both investments seemed sound and desirable.

With such happy prospects he naturally was inclined to share his good fortune, and so 'the young man's fancy lightly turned to thoughts of love'. The following letter addressed to 'Adam Wyld, Esq. Biggar' explains the situation:

Biggar. Sep. 25th, 1846.

Dear Sir,

I take the liberty of writing you a note in reference to a very important matter, which perhaps might as well have been mentioned in conversation, had not a feeling of delicacy prevented me. I believe you have already got a hint that your daughter Margaret and I have long entertained for each other a very agreeable attachment and esteem. I do not know with what feelings you may view this, but I think it right to assure you that on my part at least the attachment has not only been gradually growing but of long continuance. After the most mature deliberation I have at length made offer of marriage to her and I believe she is very willing to accept it should Mrs. Wyld and yourself be agreeable. If you be pleased to encourage me therefore, I will give a candid statement of all my circumstances and yearly income; and after knowing these, should you think it sufficiently prudent, I believe it is the desire of us both to have the affair settled as early as the necessary arrangements can be effected. Whether you be favourable to my suit or not, I trust you have too good an opinion of me to suspect that any sordid motives lie at the foundation of it. Margaret has had my affections for a long period, and did I not believe that I have hers too in such a manner as promises much happiness to us both, no other consideration whatever would induce me to give the offer which I now do. I have nothing further to add except that should you have any questions to ask before making up your mind, I promise you a faithful and candid answer. Expecting a note in reply very soon,

> I remain, Dear Sir,
> Yours truly,
> Robert Pairman.

As Maggie lived next door, frequent opportunities were afforded enabling the lovers to become thoroughly acquainted, but the marriage was not finally accomplished till 1847. The 'Happy Day' was a moving subject of debate between the betrothed. Maggie chose the merry month of May, but Robert maintained that April was by far the most favourable month – why, I wonder? – and April was chosen accordingly.

Robert, thinking to commence his new life on the very beginning of a month, suggested the first, but Maggie would have none of it; she was not going to be made an April Gowk for any man. Not she. This little episode reflects their temperaments to a tee. He was for orderly system and defiance of superstitious vagaries; she stood out for decorous custom and the good opinion of her select coterie, and of course she carried the day.

Then there was the 'providin' which was discussed to a thread by Mother and Daughter. 'But will my faither pey for a' thae things, Mother?' 'Try him!' answered the laconic and more diplomatic Madame. Both agreed, however, that not a whisper should be breathed about a piano. It might act as a bogle!

So Father and Daughter travelled one fine day by stage-coach to Glasgow to make the necessary purchases. Was he not a draper? At every counter Adam was there testing everything with careful eye and skilful hand and asking disconcerting, pertinent questions of the perplexed shopman. 'Hae ye got everything noo Marget? Dinna forget onything, ye'll never hae anither chance', and then Maggie would suddenly remember a number of things which had hitherto existed only in her head and heart and yearning maiden dreams – a psychological mystery not easily accounted for.

After all had been added up and duly liquidated, they were making for the outside door when her father with a twinkle suddenly demanded, 'Dae ye no' want a pianny?', to which the dumfoundered Maggie could only exclaim 'Oh, Faither'. But she got it, nevertheless, for which was paid £120 *argent comptant*, as her mother, who had lived in Paris, would have said. Maggie never knew her father till that auspicious day.

All preparations being now completed and the house comfortably if not luxuriously furnished, the two human filaments were woven into one strong cord which no power on earth could ever rend asunder. The marriage took place in the house of the bride's father, where were gathered a numerous company of friends and relations of both contracting parties, solemn at first but gleeful and frolicsome after the simple but impressive rite of the Relief Kirk was solemnised. Outside were the happy and irresponsible lads and lasses assembled to worship the goddess Pecunia by shouting 'Poor oot! Poor oot! Gie's a scram'le! Gie's a scram'le! Poor oot! Poor oot!', and handful after handful of pennies was sent hurtling through the expectant air. They had a royal time!

For their honeymoon the newly-wed did not charter a decorated aeroplane nor a gorgeous Rolls- Royce car nor yet 'a bicycle built for two', for these luxuries were as yet undreamt of. Not even a homely Scotch cart was requisitioned as Robert Pairman *tertius* and his heather bride had done in former days. On the other hand, intensely self-conscious, they passed on foot into Gladstone's house, amid the huzzas and congratulations mingled with the vociferous jocoseness of the hilarious guests.

During the first year of their married life a few incidents occurred which may interest their remote descendants. The bride, as a girl, had attended a Biggar school and had then been sent to a Boarding Seminary at Lanark to 'finish her off' and to acquire the genteel polish of the times. But when she became mated to an educated man and a fervid student, she was painfully aware of how little her tutors had instilled into her and she appealed to her husband to instruct her better.

To this he willingly consented and declared that he would make her 'the cleverest woman in a' Biggar'. So we can picture them o'nights deep in the study of Logic and Metaphysics, Ethics and the more perceptible 'Laws of Nature'; the teacher struck by the curious feminine intuition of the pupil and the pupil becoming more and more aware that hitherto she had been

Moving about in Worlds not realised

Their cast of mind was very similar, and as the years rolled on their mental outlook became almost identical, in fact they grew in reality into a composite soul. Some people perceived even a growing physical resemblance.

They had been married many years when one day a woman

43

at Symington Junction familiarly and confidently addressed my Mother. The latter looked surprised and inquiring, but the woman soon cleared the matter up in these words: 'Oh you don't know me, Mrs. Pairman, and I have never seen you in my life before, but you were so like "our doctor" that I felt I could not be mistaken and so I spoke to you'.

Speaking personally, I never saw any resemblance but it is significant that every individual has his or her own specific 'twinkle', the automatic spirit within acting on the involuntary primitive skin muscles of the face, and in the instance we are discussing both had a corresponding twinkle apparent to many.

But however well suited they were to each other, their married life could not escape inevitable disappointments and sorrows. One day a letter arrived announcing news that the Ayrshire Iron Company in which they were interested had failed. The following letter from Dr. David Smith, long the Minister of the Seceder Church, will explain how matters stood:

Biggar, Dec. 21st 1847.

My dear Friend,

This will be delivered to you by Dr. Pairman of this Town, a son of Mr. Pairman, my Elder. He goes to Glasgow on a very unpleasant business, namely to attend a meeting of the Shareholders of the Ayrshire Iron Company of which he is unfortunately one, to the extent of Five £20 shares. He has paid up £50 upon these, and the Committee make a demand upon him for £500 as his proportion. This he could not possibly advance as, though he is doing very well, he has been only two or three years in business and he has really nothing but his furniture. His friends will do nothing in the matter, so that unless the Committee will deal much more gently with him he must just allow the law to take its course.

The case is a very hard one for he is a very superior and deserving young man. My object in all this is to ask your advice for him, and if you could exert any influence in his behalf with any member of the Committee, to request you to do it. If they had asked £100 he might have borrowed it, but the sum demanded is for him entirely out of the question. He cannot give it nor with all his possessions realize a fourth part of it. I will take it kindly if you will give him your best counsel.

I am, my dear friend,
Yours cordially,
David Smith.

P.S. As the Railway now will soon be open, we hope to see you in Biggar.

The Railway referred to passed Symington to Carlisle but did not actually come to Biggar.

It is questionable whether this well-intentioned letter was ever presented. Those were the days before the Limited Liability Act was passed, consequently shareholders were responsible for sums far in excess of what was actually invested. I cannot now tell the sum required to obtain his discharge but in any case his furniture and belongings were valued, and what he paid left him altogether penniless. On the principle of the scalded cat, he never dabbled in shares again.

To increase the finances, Robert entered various literary competitions. One essay on the evidence of Christianity was entitled 'Sceptical Doubts Examined'. This was published in 1847 by William Oliphant and Sons and received a very favourable notice by the Press, the critics specially commending his presentment of predestination and atonement.

The identity of 'A Medical Practitioner', his *nom de guerre* on the title page, was long kept a secret under the impression that his practice would suffer if the real name of the author were disclosed. This is a curious prejudice, the people believing that a doctor who tampers with the pen is never very efficient with the stethoscope.

The following year, 1848, another great event occurred, the birth of a baby daughter whom they named **Margaret Cuth-**

**bertson** after her grandmother, wife of Adam Wyld. She brought a ray of sunshine into the home in spite of financial difficulties and disappointments. Later she became a second mother to her younger brothers and sisters and we revered her accordingly.

The 'Little Parlour', so designated because diminutiveness was one of its striking features, was the centre of our family life. It was situated at the back of the house, looking toward the sunny south and was always cosy and free from outside disturbances. The picture still is vivid. I see my father sitting in a hard wooden armchair without any cushion. My mother opposite in a low seat with a cushion indeed but destitute of arms and whose legs had been amputated at the knee. This was known as the 'nursing chair' and it frequently gave visitors the shock of their lives when they sat down with a plump on a horizontal much lower than they expected.

'Heelen' Wyld fell a victim on one occasion. When she felt herself going down and ever down she instinctively clutched at the air. This sent the chair twirling backwards and, falling with it, she found herself on the floor with her legs sticking straight up into space and her ample crinoline forming a funnel in the orthodox position for straining. It was a waefu' – some sicht and comic enough to bring tears to our eyes.

The room had a low window looking into the garden and a convenient sill or 'sole' on which to sit. This window was a great attraction to the younger members. From it we could see the stable where Ginger and Topsy were accommodated, and on the facade of the stable was an irregular row of roughly-made 'dookits'. Each pigeon had a distinctive name and a pedigree known to us better than our own. One was called the 'Conqueror' on account of its military prowess. We loved to watch their gyrations with much presumptuous wing-clapping, to criticise their coquetting and courtship and to revel in their squabbling and imperious rookity-doo-ing, ultimately leading, it may be, to an intrepid fight, sometimes to an heroic death.

# Family Life

There were few ornaments in the apartment, but cast-iron figures of Wallace and Bruce, burnished with black lead, adorned each end of the mantelpiece and attested our loyalty to Scotland's greatest heroes. These works of art, however, served also a practical purpose, for behind them were packed an untidy collection of old letters to serve as pipe-lights, till Maggie, with a leaning to spruceness, made a bonfire of the whole stock. She substituted delicate graceful spills in an artistic vase, but very soon miscellaneous letters again travelled to the custody of the 'Black Men' in defiance of Maggie's endeavours, and so the struggle continued to the end.

The weather to the country doctor is always a matter of concern, and in winter we were frequently called to witness from the window the 'Battle of the Giants' when King Sol fought King Frost for supremacy. Our opinion was asked as to the probable result, while father recounted some terrible Icelandic sagas which I have long since forgot.

But there was always a touch of poetry running through his remarks which was rich pabulum to our growing brains. When it snowed, the angels were 'casting their feathers' and when it thundered we were listening literally to the 'Voice of God'. Let all the earth keep silence before Him! When the windowpanes became frosted, the Almighty had been busy during the night tracing with consummate art the diversified forms of fern and flower, and like all his other works, though with a breath they would disappear, Behold they were very Good!

We had not much of a garden, in fact it was little better than a cottager's kailyard. There were two apple trees in its midst and the apples were of the hardest and sourest kind I have ever tasted and yet they looked enticing. What a pity the species was not conspicuous in Eden when Eve was colloguing with the Serpent! But there was an extra fine cherry tree trained on the gable of the Relief Kirk and black, red and white currant bushes between the side windows of the same edifice, the luscious berries most tantalising to the worshippers within.

Then there was a 'Burning Bush' like Moses saw in the desert. We were a little scared of this shrub and treated it with due respect, for father called it a 'Theophany' and explained that this word meant 'An appearance of God'. But with it all the garden grew magnificent vegetables and notoriously persistent weeds. Our care was to overcome these weeds, and this laborious occupation was named 'Fox-hunting'. Father encouraged us by saying, 'Take us the foxes, the little foxes that spoil the vines, for our vines have tender grapes', and upon my word we were much inspirited thereby.

These experiences occurred when we were at the make-believe stage of existence and they appealed intensely to our imagination. To be reared in such an atmosphere of poetic metaphor was indeed a genuine beatitude! And when we grew older and went to school, the parlour was where we had to learn our lessons and write our exercises. At such times nobody was allowed to speak above a whisper, but our natural passions would not always be suppressed and we then indulged in a tourney of discordant argument and futile back-chat.

'Direct Action' even was not unknown. On one such occasion Mother tried to stop the clamour but in vain. Father in his armchair was engrossed in a heavy tome and altogether unconscious of anything unusual going on. Mother begged him to interfere so he stamped with his foot and called 'Silence'. This was quite effective, but unluckily he added, 'This is not the room in which to chatter'. But Johnie instantly replied, 'In ma dictionary Parlour means a room for conversation,' which called forth a sally from Mother, 'A chip of the old block.' Needless to say, Johnie became a lawyer.

We were a very contented and united family in spite of occasional contentions physical and mental, the regrettable inheritance of original sin. But we all had great love for our parents and invariably turned to them when in any difficulty. Were there an involved Latin sentence puzzling us, or an inconceivable problem of Arithmetic to unravel, or a portion of entangled English to parse, we had just to refer to the man on the hard chair and all became as clear as crystal. Do I not well remember how he used to assert with weighty emphasis, 'Think, man, Think! What's the good of a mind if you cannot think?'

This was a word frequently used in those days. Learned men were not 'keen observers', nor 'brilliant preachers', nor 'profound metaphysicians' so much as 'Deep Thinkers'. After lessons we were encouraged to read for pleasure or profit or to amuse ourselves in an intelligent way. Sometimes Mother suggested that we should write a competitive essay and read it aloud. One subject given was 'The Moon' and Rachel came out easily first, as she always did, having more of her father's talent than the rest of us. The essay was replete with happy phrases radiating moonbeams on every side, much to the admiration of the less favoured.

We were once arguing heatedly on the question 'Is wind caused by hot air rushing into a cold stratum or the cold rushing into the hot?' The argument went on like a see-saw and our reasoning was at least emphatic if not convincing. But Mother closed the debate by saying: 'Nobody knows anything about it, Bairns. The Bible says: The wind bloweth where it listeth and thou hearest the sound thereof but canst not tell whence it cometh or whither it goeth'. We could not very well deny Scripture nor contradict our parent, but was this not an Argumentum ad Populum or some other form of illegitimate Logic?

We felt there was an artful fallacy somewhere, but Johnie was not present to advocate our cause so we remained squashed. Our Mother was very ingenuous with her quotations though we did not always perceive the pertinency of them, which raised an amused smile on our father's face, who however remained silent.

She was a clever woman nevertheless and had a wonderful memory. She could repeat long screeds of prose or poetry done sometimes to shame us when we complained of our Memory exercise. 'Toots man, that's nothing. When I was a girl I had to learn far longer extracts than that.'

Then she would declaim, as if from a pulpit, stanza after stanza of 'Paradise Lost' without a blunder. Or she would expatiate on the great Chalmers who used to preach from the Burn Braes, just under the Moat Knowe near Daft Jennie's cottage and never looked at book or scrip for over an hour. Then she would imitate the matchless orator by reciting, almost without a breath, part of one of his sermons which she had heard as a girl on the school green:

> It matters not as to the substantive amount of the suffering, whether it be dictated by the hardness of the heart or permitted by the heedlessness of the mind, in either case it stands true that the archdevourer Man stands out in bold pre-eminence,
> AN ANIMAL OF PREY

How she dirled the phrases, especially the last one, into the air, with impressive gestures! She was not like the woman from Elsrickle who walked into Biggar one day to hear Thomas Chalmers preach. On her return the neighbours inquired of her how she liked the noted orator. She replied, 'Oh, he swat and he reekit and he reekit and swat and he dichtit his broo and he reekit again and the great big moothfu's o' graun', graun' words was something terrible a'thegither'!

On Sunday nights we all assembled in the little parlour to be put through our Catechism and to receive further instruction in Bible Truth. This was the most delightful hour of the whole week. From our earliest years we had breathed its atmosphere and had absorbed, as our capacity permitted, the transcendent influences at work. We left far behind us the sordid world, with its worries and puerile interests, and concentrated our minds and our hearts on the Unseen.

Father had a marvellous way with children and adolescents and drew such vivid pictures of Life and its Eternal Verities, and with such earnestness and such appropriate metaphor that we became literally fascinated. He himself seemed transformed into a Superior Being. We knew and loved him as our Earthly father, but somehow, on these occasions, he was different and we realised that 'the light upon his face shone from the windows of another world'.

This was the best possible argument for the reality of the Realms beyond and it sank into our hearts never to be obliterated. He had a special word for each of us, intended to suit the peculiar pattern of our varied dispositions: Maggie with her domestic instincts, Robert with his sporting propensities, Adam with his tender-heartedness, Johnie with his love of Nature, Rachel with her desire for proofs, Tommy with his argumentative proclivities, and Nancy with her pliability and sweet irenic virtues. All received their share of Spiritual Food; all drank freely of the Water of Life. And Mother, sitting on the nursing-chair and regarding us intently, would whisper: 'No man shall pluck them out of my hand'.

Here were unity, joy, happiness, assurance of the future and contentment. And yet they say that Calvinism is a hard religion and induces gloom and depression! Those who say so know nothing whatever about it.

After this grouping on the Mount of Transfiguration and before we separated for the night, Father would gently tap on the chimneypiece and call up the 'lum' – 'Cheepie Birdy, Cheepie Birdy! Have you anything for the little ones tonight?' In answer we distinguished a very faint 'Yes' in the bleating tone of aegophony. Those most prejudiced echoed in unison 'Yes! Yes!'

'Are you sure it did not say "No"?' queried father with twinkling eye. 'It said "Yes, Yes" I heard it quite plain.' So sweeties were brought from the wee shop and distributed to the just and unjust amid much contented ebullition of fun and merriment. Such was commonly our little innocent pleasantry dear to our hearts.

We called these lozenges our 'bird' and went to bed with sweetness in our marrow and in our mouths. Did this custom connect us with the Auld Franco-Scottish Alliance? Cheepie-birdy would then be 'chapeau borde', a cocked hat, presented as a distinction to the deserving. Ah me, can we never get away from Tradition's whims?

In these family gatherings we felt, like Peter, that it was good for us to be here, and would fain have erected permanent tabernacles. But do not the Arabs tell us that 'All sunshine makes the desert', and it would seem immaterial whether this sunshine be a present emanation or the effulgence of a million years ago bottled up in peat and coal and let loose again by a domestic Spunkie. So we children had to rise willy-nilly,

> And face with an undaunted tread
> The long black passage up to bed!

while Father – how we pitied him – had often, very often indeed, to obey an urgent call and encounter the cold inclement inky night to ride, booted and spurred, far away to the distant hills.

Never a grumble escaped him but when commiserated he would simply say 'It was to this that I was called'. To me at any rate it was unspeakably pathetic and the pathos did not end here. Mother, ever troubled for his welfare and comfort, passed weary hours at the nursery window waiting and worrying for her good man, more especially when the roads were slippery or the Tweed was in flood, necessitating his swimming the river. I do not think she ever forgot that winter's night on the Staneheid Road where he lay for many hours broken and perishing. Happy she when was heard in the distance the steady decided hoof-beat of faithful Ginger.

Now, many years later, when my susceptible memory turns to the old house, it always comes to rest in that little parlour.

# 7

# THE WEE SHOP

Let me turn aside to relate some trivialities which may touch a sympathetic chord in the minds of Robert's descendants. We shall begin with a diminutive room, some twelve feet or so square, situated on the left-hand when you have entered the house by the front door. Coming in from the street, your attention was at once arrested by a variety of commingling odours, creating a persistent, satisfying, dreamy pleasure. These proceeded from the 'wee shop' whose multi-tinted glassy walls I recall with a feeling akin to reverence. This tiny apartment had two windows, the one looking across the street, above which was a small sign-board bearing in chaste gold letters the words

**PAIRMAN SURGEON.**

The other window, looking up the street, had another sign-board on top, whereon was printed, also in gold letters but larger, the one descriptive word

**LABORATORY.**

To our young imaginative minds this was no common every-day shop, but a Temple of Learning, Philosophy and Science. It was full of mysteries and recondite influences, an emporium of strange powers and bottled arcana. Its atmosphere directed the mind to classic Greece and Rome, to Egypt, Arabia and the Tropical Isles of the Sea!

To have served at its Altar meant a permanent urge to

organised Ambition. Of the seven boys who presided over its destiny, three became medical men, one a medical student, two became chemists and one a Solicitor before the Supreme Courts.

The first was Thomas Pairman, a younger brother of my father, who was inordinately modest and conscientious, industrious and aspiring. He had a terrible fondness for Pontefract Cakes and Gelatin Lozenges, the latter slippery, dangerous, tasteless things which had a great partiality for sliding down the throat or windpipe without giving due notice. But Tom would not dream of helping himself to one without obtaining leave, though often told to take as many as he liked at any time.

He began his career as a medical student but died at the early age of 21. My Mother on one occasion spoke of my father as being 'clever', which only distressed him and he remarked, 'Don't say that, Margaret, I never could hold the candle to my brother Tom'. I think this knowledge must have kept him humble.

The following were the seven acolytes who served and passed on: Thomas Pairman, already mentioned; Dr. Andrew Brown, London; Aaron Whitfield, Chemist, Biggar; my three elder brothers and myself.

When I was about 11 or 12 years old, my brother John became articled to **Mr. John Buchan, Writer, Peebles,** and went to live there. Consequently the torch was handed on to me. My father, the impelling genius of the whole establishment, was very fond of applying Classical or Biblical names to those with whom he was most familiar. The name of his horse was really 'Ginger', but when out driving he facetiously addressed it as Abimelech, and somehow the name seemed to suit it.

So when I was installed as major-domo, he christened me 'Wee Socrates' because I was now an apothecary and greatly addicted to answering questions by asking others. This must have been irritating to a degree, but his gentle disposition enabled him to suffer fools gladly and I was greatly enriched thereby.

He frequently spoke of Ancient Greek heroes in a light whimsical vein, and I learned that Thales of Miletus reckoned that everything was made of water 'like some doctors' prescriptions, only it is then called Aqua Fontana'. I discovered that the curious twirl seen on prescriptions meant 'By Jupiter' or 'Hocus Pocus' and had a great virtue in it 'equal to that of a doctor's trumpet'.

He told me the pitiful story of the ill-starred Socrates drinking the lethal Hemlock, which aroused a fascinating interest in the Conium bottle and made me take extra care in measuring out the doses. Then there was Dover's Powder, and I wished to learn why it was associated with the famous seaport.

He told me there once lived a Dr. Dover who was also a master-mariner and who had the good fortune to rescue Alexander Selkirk, marooned on the Island of Juan Fernandez. When ashore he held medical consultations in a London coffee-house, and made a great name for himself by prescribing, in the treatment of fevers, what is now familiar to everybody, 'Dover's Powder'. One day he met Daniel Defoe and related to him his adventure with Selkirk the castaway, and Defoe was so interested in the yarn that, with the pen of genius, he composed *Robinson Crusoe*, a story loved by boys of all nationalities.

But my first experience of his penchant for the ancient somebodies occurred when I was five years old or so. There had been a heavy fall of snow. Wrapped up in the tanned skin of a black curly retriever dog, hair outside, I was rolling along an enormous snowball to place on the summit of a half-made snowman when I heard behind me my father's voice saying 'You're a perfect little Hercules'.

I did not know who Hercules was, but I was confident he must be a commendable individual and felt puffed up accordingly. I had placed a plank of wood against the incipient man

1. Robert Pairman (1818-1873) as a medical student. Painted by his uncle, John Pairman.

2. Robert Pairman the grocer (1784-1867), father of Dr. Pairman. Painted in 1838, probably by John Pairman.

3. Rachel Davidson (1784-1833), first wife of Robert Pairman senior. She was the daughter of John and Joan Davidson of Mitchelhill Kilbucho.

4. Nancy Pairman, the doctor's much-loved sister who died in 1834 at the age of 17. Painted by her uncle, John Pairman.

5. Adam Pairman (1820-1900), brother of Dr. Pairman. First manager of the Biggar branch of the National Bank of Scotland.

6. Agnes Fletcher Brown, Mrs Adam Pairman, who died in 1930 aged 93.

7. Jeannie (Jessie) Watson, who married Dr. Pairman's son, Dr. Robert Pairman.

8. Robert Miller SSC (1876-1971) with his Grannie Pairman (Dr. Pairman's widow). Taken about 1880.

9. Biggar Bowling Club, 1859. Dr Pairman is seated left of centre, wearing a light-coloured tile hat. The third figure to the right of him, rather shrunken, is his father, also Robert Pairman.

10. Biggar, 1861. Dr Pairman's first home after his marriage was in the last building seen on the left-hand side of the street, just to the left of the gas lamp globe. On the right-hand side of the street, old Robert Pairman's successor in business is standing at the shop door. The hill in the background is Tinto.

11. Family group, about 1917, showing Robert Pairman Miller with his wife Helen Tweedie and their children, Sarah, John, Margaret and Richard.

12. All that remained in 1994 of Mitchelhill, once the home of Dr. Pairman's mother, Rachel Davidson, and later the childhood home of his daughter-in-law Jessie Watson. The farmhouse (now demolished) was to the right of these buildings.

13. The Pairmans' house in Biggar today.

but when I tried to roll the snow-ball up the inclined plane to complete his torso, I could not get it to go over the top. On the contrary, the moment I withdrew my support it rolled down again, making fruitless my perspiring efforts.

Again the same voice announced that I was no Hercules after all, but only a 'Cissy Fuss'. The only Cissy I knew was Cissy Ormiston, a mere girl and not very good-looking at that. I felt offended at being considered no better than a lassie, and the notion rankled in my masculine mind.

But years afterwards when I was spouting Virgil at the Parish School I came to the line 'ingens et non exsuperabile saxum' (a great and unwieldy stone). It was then that I realised to my surprise that Cissy Fuss was spelt 'Sisyphus' and that he was a man condemned to forced labour indeed. But still he was a man, and that was something superior to a wee lassie! And I often thought that a growing snowball would have been more difficult to roll anywhere than a big stone would be, till I remembered that the honourable gentleman was in Hell, and that most assuredly the snowball would have melted.

But my whole time was not occupied with merely asking questions and absorbing entertaining stories of the heroic age. There was work to do and that work to be done with meticulous care and probity, under the keen and vigilant eye of a professional man. The career was a magnificent and profitable training not only in simples and compounds but in perseverance, integrity and precision. Do I not remember well the accuracy with which Magnesia, Rhubarb and Ginger were first mixed in a mortar with pestle and then passed through a very fine-meshed hair sieve with pliant spatula to make Gregory's Mixture, filling the shop and my own lungs with pungent unpalatable dust.

After spending an hour at this performance it was somewhat galling when the doctor tumbled out the whole lot onto a large sheet of dark blue paper. Woe betide if a single speck of white stood out against the blue, for the whole long process had to be gone over again from the very beginning. No scamp work permitted in those bejan halcyon days!

The making of compound Colocynth Pills left a flavour of Bitter Aloes on the palate for a week! The shaping of a horse-bolus was a work of art, with beautiful lines like those of Phidias. A Gibbons Pill was a disgrace. When the Spirit of Mindererus was being made, some boy friends were usually admitted to see the process. A big glass measure was filled with Acetic Acid and a solid lump of Carbonate of Ammonia was dropped into it, the result being a great disturbance of the fluid and a fierce emission of bubbles which made the top boil like a very cauldron.

To increase the wonder the doctor called it a Volcano or Burning Mountain, and we viewed it with feelings of awe and veneration. We understood that **Tinto Hill** in the dreamy distance was such another volcano, and might renew its activity at any moment, so Tinto for a time was regarded with suspicion.

Then there was the reduction of Strong Sulphuric Acid into a medicinal form, accomplished by taking a long glass beaker of water and adding the acid to it drop by drop at not too frequent intervals. We were cautioned that if too much acid were added at one time, the beaker might crack from the great heat evolved by chemical action. I may say that this is quite true for I have tried it. What normal boy wouldn't? 'Prove all things.'

From the end window of the laboratory we had a splendid view of the wide street and could observe all the events accruing without being ourselves seen, and on Market and Fair days we never tired of watching the moving rarieshow. Half-way up the side window was a shelf on which stood two large carboys – pink and blue – in which reflections of passers-by were visible. These reflections increased or diminished according as the promenaders approached or receded, the effect being a phantasmagoria of humanity bobbing up and down, growing or dwindling in the fluid medium – a primitive Kinematograph.

## The Wee Shop

To the philosophic mind they were nearer the noumena than the phenomena; they were a puzzle of Being; they were a natural charade. A farmer's wife one day glued her eyes on this fantastic scene and blurted out in horror 'Megstie-me, doctor, dae ye keep wee bairns in a bottle?' Then excitedly 'Good God! doctor, are they . . . are they . . . leevin'?'

At the back of a crimson curtain were a number of Natural History specimens, among which were several 'serpents' or adders preserved in soda water bottles. We used to think they came from folks' insides but as a matter of fact they were caught at Clarencefield in Dumfriesshire by Adam Wyld when a boy at school.

The customers and their requirements were a source of great amusement to me, and in the absence of the Doctor I prescribed for them to the best of my ability. The former made me quite familiar not only with medical dog-Latin but with the popular names of drugs consecrated by the learning and superstition of ages. I might be asked for 'Healin' and drawin' Sa', 'Seerup o' Squirrels', 'Draygon's Bluid', 'An unce o' Berks', 'Speceefic 'ntment for ma faither' 'Luck- wid Lotion for a beilin' thoomb', 'Draps for sair sen', 'Something guid for the yeuk – we ae hae it', 'A poother for the wean, the doctor kens the age himsel', 'Twae leeches for a flamin' knee', and so on, and so on.

The leeches were kept in a white porcelain jar with perforated lid. By their behaviour we could forecast the weather; if they hugged the bottom of the jar it would soon rain; if they clung to the lid we were sure of a dry spell.

Two curios in the wee shop interested us greatly; one was a book written wholly in Latin, entitled *Conspectus Medicinae Theoreticae*. This was by Dr. James Gregory, of Gregory's Mixture fame, and was one of the doctor's class-books at College.

The other curio was a small deepish brass plate with an oval piece of the lip circumference cut away to fit the arm when blood-letting was going on. Phlebotomy was very much in vogue when my father began practice, but he was never fully convinced of its general utility, and after being bled himself he discarded it altogether. This was when he was a little over ten years in practice when one winter evening he was riding down the Staneheid Road, which is paved with the living rock, and his horse slipped and fell on him, breaking his thigh. It was an intensely cold, frosty night and he lay helpless till found by a neighbour in the morning.

He was carried home and old Dr. Kello attended to the fracture, but acute pneumonia setting in, he deemed it advisable to perform venesection and a good many ounces of blood were drawn. This may have prevented further complications and limited the pneumonia, but the patient was greatly reduced in condition and took years to regain strength. This experience consigned the Barber-Surgeon's plate to the Antiquarian Museum.

On Market days and Fair days, our house was as busy and stirring as a hotel bar. Prosperous gentlemen-farmers who had feathered their nests during the Crimean War, and Scotch-plaided shepherds smelling of heather, with chiselled, poetic faces and carrying their artistic crooks, made their way uninvited to the little parlour 'ben the hoose', to ca' the crack with the Doctor and with each other.

The room was generally full of tobacco smoke, the pipe of peace being handed round the company, the Doctor taking care always to begin the process by a few hearty puffs. This custom, perhaps not very hygienic, was quite the practice in those days and considered a token of genial sodality.

Those requiring medical examination and advice were taken to the dining room and afterwards to the wee shop to have their prescriptions dispensed. It was marvellous how the Doctor flitted about amongst them with his friendly sallies, yet maintaining his professional dignity, and it was marvellous also to see the reverence and esteem with which he was regarded by them all.

He was no charlatan nor Merry Andrew, however. He

# The Wee Shop

could be serious enough when the occasion required, and whatever he said was always well-considered and accepted implicitly. He had a very placid, contemplative, sober mien, but underneath this repose was a vast fund of wit and humour, sparkling and kindly.

When my brother John laid aside the pestle and mortar at Biggar to ply the quill on a three-legged stool at Peebles, he found the exchange exceedingly dull and enervating. In a crisis of distress he at last unburdened his soul in a long letter home, complaining that all he had to stimulate him was scribbling wills and writing decrees against salmon-poachers on the Tweed, to him a dismal, insipid, witless occupation at the best.

I also received a letter from him inquiring about everything and everybody. The letter ended in rhyme and I got my father to answer it in equal terms, a task in which he never found any difficulty. This is the reply which I copied and sent:

> Our Johnie lad, we're very sure;
>   since you are now from home
> That you will be most glad to hear;
>   from Robert and from Tom.
> Robert you know your cousin is;
>   across the street he dwells,
> Tho' sometimes to assist wee Tom;
>   the pills and powders sells.
> In mortar we do pound and grind;
>   the plastic mass to make,
> Until with nasty sticky hands
>   we to the well betake.
> And then, with pens and books and slates;
>   our meanings and our grammar,
> We try into each other's heads;
>   some learned stuff to hammer.
> For well ye ken that tasks ill-learned;
>   and said wi' hums and haws

## A Scottish Country Doctor

Bring down the Master's sulky brows;
    and still more horrid tawse.
For losh man Johnie wha can tell;
    but we may yet turn law-men,
And scribble wills and write decrees;
'gainst folk that catch the sauman!
    Noo Johnie tae our cousins a';
    sae sweet they are and fair, man,
Gae kindest love and mony a kiss;
    frae Bob and Tommy Pairman.

There is no doubt that this verse would have cheered the homesick brother, for it was evident that his heart was still in the wee shop in Biggar.

# 8

# BIGGAR, 'A TOWN
# OF LIGHT AND LEADING'

Biggar, even in the Primitive School days, claimed to be 'a town of light and leading'. There were many men with well balanced minds in the district, capable of expressing themselves in language pithy and ornate. Among others was Scott the Dominie already referred to, who was endowed with high attainments as a scholar and who got the Parish School appointment in competition with the celebrated Dr. Carson, afterwards Rector of the Royal High School of Edinburgh.

The various Ministers, especially Mr. Christison, were far above the average in intelligence and literary gifts and well-versed in letters. Many averred that he should have been a Professor of Literature and Belles-Lettres in a University, so scholarly and polished were his sermons and addresses.

But the common people also, educated at John Knox's Parish Schools, displayed a true appreciation of good expression and poetic thought. In fact there seemed to be a wave of intellectual power at that time passing over the district, and many remarked it then and since. This may have been due to the influence of Sir Walter Scott's novels, the propaganda of the passionate Chartists, Tom Paine and his Age of Reason, the contrecoup of the French Revolution, or possibly all these causes combined, acting of course on a solid basis evolved by long years of undisturbed isolation and contemplation.

Little wonder then that the Biggar Scientific Institute came into being. Periodic lectures were delivered and discussed, the criticism being often more racy and entertaining, certainly more spontaneous and humorous, than the lecture itself. William Pillans, beforehand with tuck of drum, paraded the town and announced in grandiloquent terms the subject of address, finishing with the savoury 'Persons no' members wull be admitted by peyin' tippence each. God save the Queen!'

This Society had a fairly long life as such country organisations go, but in 1854 it was superseded by the Athenaeum which continued giving lectures, and like the former society, had in connection with it a Reading-Room and Library.

It was under the aegis of the Athenaeum that Dr. John Brown, himself a Biggar boy, presented to the world his touching story 'Rab and his Friends' and it inspired a variety of critical remarks characteristic of the individuals who indulged in them. But it was rather disturbing and unbalancing to many who expected something deeper and more scientific from a metropolitan physician.

My father, who presided over the meeting, in thanking Dr. Brown for his address, said there was more in the paper than was at first apparent, and he felt confident that one day they would see it in print. On the way home Miss Jackson pronounced it 'Just a little prose poem', while Lowrie Pillans, with an impatient toss of the head grunted 'Auch, it was only aboot wheen dowgs!'

One of the most frequent contributors to the Scientific Institute and Athenaeum was Robert Pairman, the young surgeon. We find that in the earlier years of his practice he gave a series of 'Essays on Popular Physiology', the last of which was 'The Function of Absorption' following that on 'The Function of Digestion', the former of which is the only one to survive time and negligence.

Like Moses, Paul, Demosthenes and some other distinguished men, Robert was afflicted, as the reader already knows, with a particularly exasperating 'thorn in the flesh'. Afraid that this stumbling block might militate against the success of their delivery, he got the schoolmaster of Glenholm, reputed an excellent reader, to take his place on the platform. When the last paper was being read and acting on 'information received', the Author, unseen, ensconced himself behind a curtain near the door and could scarcely recognise his own composition on account of the stilted and pedantic manner of the country dominie. He at once resolved that in future he would deliver his papers himself, whatever betide.

The theme of his next dissertation was Asiatic Cholera, a topic of intense interest among the savants all over Europe at that time and one on which no two were in accord. This was in 1856. His former attempts could lay no claim to originality, but contained merely plain statements of well-ascertained scientific facts, the chief merit of the papers being simplicity and clearness of style and shrewd aptness in illustration. But this Cholera address was of quite a different standard and reflected very careful investigation and acute, almost brilliant, reasoning. I shall have more to say about this later on.

The lecture undoubtedly brought his name prominently before the public, and he got several offers of a remunerative medical appointment to large industrial works in Glasgow, Airdrie, Lancashire, &c., but to all these he turned a deaf ear. When referring to those days, he used to say that he preferred the mountain air of Biggar and freedom, to a polluted atmosphere and a practice limited by conditions.

But in 1858 he was thunderstruck when one day he was proffered a Bank Agency in Biggar itself. The National Bank of Scotland intended to open a branch and was very insistent on Dr. Pairman's filling the position of manager, with the right to practise Medicine as well. All the directors desired was to have his name appear as their accredited Agent, and to be responsible for a substitute, if he employed one.

The offer was a very tempting one and its acceptance would free him from many a solitary midnight ride among the cold bleak hills; he could limit his practice to his own desires; he could claim a good salary and a rent-free house, and what with Banking and Medicine combined he would be in a fair way to make a competency.

But he was of a more altruistic disposition. At that time his brother Adam was a draper in Biggar, whose health was causing his friends some anxiety. Thinking that banking would be a more suitable occupation for him, entailing shorter hours and more amenities, he declined with gratitude the Bank's kind offer, but strongly recommended Adam. He also suggested that they make him sole agent, and so it eventuated, to the gratification of all concerned.

The Bank was opened December 1st 1858. My uncle Adam was a genial man of gentle disposition, thoroughly honest, capable and conscientious, and as the years rolled on he made a magnificent success of the banking venture. His younger son, William Brown Pairman, succeeded him, and retired in 1929 after a long and prosperous term of office.

**Dr. Richard Mackenzie**, a celebrated Edinburgh surgeon and Lecturer on Surgery in one of its schools, often came to visit his brother John Ord Mackenzie at Dolphinton. Richard is still known in the surgical world as the originator of 'Mackenzie's modification of Syme's amputation'. On one occasion my father was called to a lady patient at Dolphinton whose symptoms were very puzzling. The diagnosis resolved itself into a question of mere adiposity or serious dropsy, and he decided it was the former and pronounced accordingly.

Naturally Dr Mackenzie heard of the perplexing case on his brother's estate and took the liberty (against professional rules) of examining the patient for himself. He had however the courtesy to write my father, acquainting him with what he had done.

In this letter he said that he disagreed altogether with the diagnosis and asked for a consultation which was readily granted. Both examined the patient. Mackenzie maintained that it was cardiac disease and dropsy; Pairman said it was simply fat. The arguments brought to bear on either side were keen and subtle, but at last Mackenzie acknowledged gracefully the correctness of the original diagnosis and they parted the best of friends. In fact this little episode created a firm and enduring fellowship, and the friendship of Damon and Pythias, of David and Jonathan, was not more real, staunch, and mutual than that between the town and country surgeons.

After this, they frequently met and enjoyed many a medical discussion and brotherly contest. One day they got arguing about the principles of fracture treatment. Mackenzie got quite a shock when Pairman advocated early movement of the tendons and joints to make a complete success. The usual practice was to keep the joints immediately above and below the fracture perfectly rigid for weeks, the result being often a stiff or ankylosed joint; whereas judicious and controlled movement during the healing process kept the parts free and supple from the very first.

Mackenzie was surprised and greatly interested, and asked for a demonstration on an actual case. Pairman was able to do this on a number of patients undergoing treatment at all stages, which fully convinced Mackenzie that the method was reasonable and the result excellent. The city surgeon was also greatly amused at the improvised splints which his country brother was obliged to adopt, e.g. the kitchen tongs and poker, padded with straw or heather, the 'reenge' or pot cleaner, the good-wife's knitting-sheath or other domestic apparatus which, though effective, contrasted strangely with the beautifully-turned appliances of a well-furnished hospital.

When next Mackenzie gave a lecture on the treatment of fractures, he quoted the methods of a number of acknowledged authorities who all advocated the application of rigid splints. The lecturer then added impressively, 'But Dr. Pairman of Biggar removes the splints every few days, protects the fracture itself with his hands and carefully and methodically practises passive movement of the joints and tendons thereby preventing adhesions becoming organised and, as I can personally testify, with most excellent results'. At this lecture were two smiling Biggar youths who became gleg as weasels when they heard the name 'Biggar'. These were John and Alexander Kello, who were then students of Medicine and who ultimately practised for many years as confrères of my father.

In the year 1854 the tragic and deplorable Crimean War broke out and nothing would satisfy Mackenzie but to go out as a surgeon to the troops. Here he devoted himself so well to his work that among his soldier friends he became an actual hero. At the gallant taking of the Redan he attended to the wounded several days without resting night or day.

Nature however has her limit of endurance and called out insistently for sleep, and at last he staggered almost automatically to his tent. With features drawn, collapsed, haggard and bloody, minus a cap and in his shirt sleeves, he found himself passing in front of some thousands of soldiers drawn up in battle array. These recognised the surgeon and knew of the merciful work in which he had been engaged, and regardless of discipline and holding aloft their busbies and helmets on their bayonet points they cheered and cheered him to the echo.

Mackenzie was scarcely able to acknowledge their salute. Alas, it was his last oration! That same night Asiatic Cholera found a ready victim in Mackenzie, who rapidly succumbed to its fatal thrust. Nature had her desire for sleep, sleep that knew no waking.

When the news reached Biggar, my father was greatly moved and for many days went about his work mourning as for a brother. In fact the occurrence created a crisis in his life. Why was this brilliant young man, so full of goodness, so intelligent, so hopeful of the future, thus in the Spring-time of his days suddenly blotted out? God indeed moves in a mysterious way.

Before enlisting with the troops Mackenzie left his only daughter in charge of his friend Pairman who frequently visited her at Dolphinton.

## Biggar, 'A Town of Light and Leading'

Years passed, my father had gone to his last long rest, the girl had grown up and left the district when one day John Ord Mackenzie called on my Mother, who inquired 'Where is your niece now?' The uncle answered, 'She was left well off and had a good home with me but in spite of my remonstrances and entreaties she became a nurse in a London Hospital and devoted her life to that calling. Nothing would keep her at home'. That is so, the inherited urge was too vehement.

# 9

# ASIATIC CHOLERA

Even amongst the highest medical authorities there was no clear conception of the true nature of Asiatic Cholera, and the treatment was equally empiric, contradictory and haphazard. The features of the disease were certainly most perplexing. Dr Pairman enumerates them as follows:

1. Characteristic symptoms of an individual case.
2. Prevailing diarrhoea in affected districts.
3. The cause seems sometimes to reside in wells.
4. It follows the track of a great river.
5. Medical men escape – sick nurses fall.
6. Runs along one side of a street only.
7. In a workhouse it may select victims from one sex.
8. Strange sights in the sky over affected districts.
9. Electric telegraphs and magnets lose their power.
10. Rarely ascends mountains.
11. Prevails in marshy districts, seaport towns, etc.
12. Can travel against the wind.
13. A thunderstorm suddenly arrests it.

Here then was a Chinese jigsaw puzzle to unravel. Whatever the cause may be, it must account for all those features. He was in search of 'one single cause' which would not only account for these phenomena but harmonise them into one consistent whole.

When he arrived at a definite decision he happened to meet Professor Syme in consultation and asked him abruptly, 'What is your opinion of the cause of cholera?' Syme answered, 'My candid opinion is that nobody knows anything at all about it'. My father then expressed succintly the views he held and the treatment he had elaborated. Syme listened very attentively, cogitated a few minutes, and then exclaimed, 'I see no flaw whatever in your argument and it is quite new to me'. He added, 'You are a clever fellow, Pairman. Why don't you come to Town?' But that is another story.

Dr Pairman's Cholera Lecture to the Athenaeum in 1856 was received with great enthusiasm. It was delivered without a hiatus of speech (most unexpected by the lecturer) and it was unanimously agreed to ask the author to have it published. It soon appeared in pamphlet form dedicated thus:

To
Alexander Dundas Ross Cochrane Wishart Baillie, President
The Rev. John Christison, A.M. Vice-President
and the Remaining Members of the Biggar Athenaeum
This Lecture
Delivered in their hearing and published at their request
is inscribed by The Author.
Biggar, April 25, 1856.

The pamphlet was well reviewed: 'A clever and well-written address' (*The Scotsman*); 'A valuable contribution to science and to Society itself' (*The Glasgow Citizen*); 'In the pamphlet before us a clear view is to be obtained of the steps of that slow but apparently simple process by which at length we have arrived at something like definite conclusions regarding the cause or causes of cholera, the manner of its propagation and spread and the means, fortunately very effectual, likely to arrest the march of its future invasions' (*The Caledonian Mercury*); 'This treatise contains much valuable and interesting information' (*The Kelso Chronicle*); 'We commend Mr. Pairman's Lecture as an accurate exposé of the latest views of this disease' (*The Edinburgh Medical Journal*).

The consequences of this publication were varied and

certainly not anticipated. Many requests reached him to deliver a lecture on any subject he pleased to such and such a Literary Society or Science Club. Even Lockerbie craved a crumb. In fact he was guaranteed a handsome sum by a professional agent to tour the country delivering addresses. All these proposals, however, he definitely declined.

Perhaps to the author the most pleasing fruit of the Cholera pamphlet was a letter from the Rev. George Scott of the Glasgow City Mission, an extract from which I may be permitted to quote:

> A few days ago I fell in with an admirable lecture you have lately published on Asiatic Cholera. The views set forth seem so original and striking and so commend themselves to common sense that it appears to me you have struck the nail on the head and that henceforth you will rank among the benefactors of your race.

The letter then proposes that he should write a few booklets to distribute among the masses of the people instructing them on the benefits of good ventilation, cleanliness and sanitation generally; also how to resist infection from fevers, then very prevalent, and on the principles and methods of disinfection.

In a succeeding letter, the Reverend gentleman continues:

> Accomplish this and you will have done that which will entitle you to the lasting gratitude of your countrymen. Thousands perish every year from ignorance of these things.

It may be well to remind the reader that this was a new venture. Such a method intended to ameliorate the deplorable conditions of slumdom had practically never been tried before. But it agreed exactly with the trend of my father's ambition. On my last visit to Scotland an old lady remarked to me that 'His whole efforts were devoted to the welfare of the people', so he entered into the task with zest and earnestness. The results were four tracts of eight pages each, entitled respectively:

1. Infection: How to deal with it in the Sick-Chamber.
2. Dirt and Overcrowding in Dwellings of the Poor.
3. Fever Poisons: How to make them in the City.
4. Infection: How to resist its Power.

The tracts are expressed in simple yet pithy terms and practical withal. Some of the descriptions amount to real good literature, the product of a proficient and facile pen. His vivid picture of a Typhus Fever patient is most arresting, and other passages are equally clear and talented.

The tracts came under the eye of **Dr. George Combe**, one of the first and for long the most eminent of the Sanitary and Public Health advocates in Britain, who included quotations from them in his new edition of 'Religion and Science'.

Miss Brewster, a celebrated writer at that time, in one of her books also made extracts which attracted the attention of the Committee of the Council of Education, who requested the author to permit excerpts from them for educational purposes. I remember seeing in an old school book a few of these by 'A clever country surgeon'. One was:

A necessary consequence of bad ventilation in the home is bad morality and a strong temptation into the paths of vice. In other words, fresh air is not only conducive to health and vigour but to virtue and religion. For without pure air even the richest food cannot nourish, and the carbon of the blood cannot burn. Consequently impurity of air induces thinness and coldness of blood. Coldness of blood creates shivering and discomfort and these again a craving for something that will light up throughout the body a feeling of warmth. The intoxicating cup readily presents itself, and for the sake of its short-lived genial glow many, alas, yield themselves to its fatal spell. So true is it that all efforts to improve the working classes must comprehend improvement in the construction of their dwellings – that cleanliness is the handmaid of temperance and religion – and that sanitary reform, conducing alike to elevate the tone of public health and public morality, is not more a philanthropic act than a Christian duty.

All this was very delightful to the author. Many thousands of copies were distributed by Sanitary Associations throughout the country, resulting in the amelioration of the wretched conditions under which the masses existed and a definite uplift of the people themselves. After the author had long entered into his rest, another edition was printed in 1878 'by the consent of Dr. Pairman's family'.

Permit me now to amplify the remarks already made on Asiatic Cholera by describing from the pamphlet the characteristic symptoms of an actual case:

1. The patient presents an extremely emaciated appearance, his fixed glassy eyes languidly looking out from far within their hollow sockets.
2. Incessant vomiting and diarrhoea have reduced life to the very lowest ebb yet his restless frame knows no repose.
3. He is tossed about in all the sufferings of cramp.
4. The circulation is almost at a standstill with consequent cyanosis and frigidity. His face has a blackish or blue appearance and every feature shrunk in the extreme. You put your hand upon his pulseless wrist, it is cold as the touch of lifeless clay.
5. The man's consciousness and mental faculties remain entire. He attempts to speak to you and on bending down your ear to catch the sound you are startled by a cold sensation striking on your cheek. It is his icy breath issuing from his lungs as frosty air would issue from an icehouse.
6. His normal secretions are in abeyance. He is totally unable to shed a tear.

## Asiatic Cholera

Surely this is a strange disease! The only instance perhaps in Nature where acute suffering, conscious of its agony, cannot weep, the only suffering which the power of Opium cannot mitigate, the only exhaustion which the power of stimulants cannot touch.

In seeking to explain the different symptoms and discover the true cause and origin of this mysterious disease, one is more or less swayed by the theories already existing. At the time the pamphlet was published the author found himself in a perfect maelstrom of whirling opinions. The older practitioners decided, without fear of contradiction, that the cause was an Epidemic Influence operating in the atmosphere. Another group maintained that it was due to noxious vapours or miasmata rising from the ground. Some contended 'there may be diffused through the atmosphere some Noxious Fluid, the subtlety and minuteness of which has hitherto eluded the grasp of chemical analysis'. Once more, some medical men of superior standing intimated that the true cause may be myriads of minute invisible insects.

One enthusiastic medico was so convinced of the truth of this theory and conceiving that these insects must be larger in the upper strata of the atmosphere took a trip one day in a balloon to catch and dissect some of then. Whether or not he took with him an entomologist's net is not recorded. Professor Schonbeen of Germany put forward the suggestion that 'the choleraic poison might consist of minute and invisible Vegetable effluvia (or fungi as they are called) formed in the atmosphere, in consequence of a disturbed condition of electric action'. This bald announcement Father read in a daily newspaper without any comment emanating either from the professor himself or from any one else.

But the idea pleased, or as they would now say, intrigued him, and the main part of the pamphlet is devoted to the furthering of this principle. But something else was wanted. How did these effluvia act? He could find no reference to this question in the medical literature at his command, nor could he derive any information from any of his medical brethren in the metropolis. So, he was thrown back on his own deliberations.

After very careful cogitation, he concluded that, whether fungi were the origin of the disease or not, it was at least something that acted on the digestive tract as a 'drastic hydragogue cathartic'; that this something was alive and multiplied in this tract only, that is to say the poison never entered the blood at all, consequently the infection was to be found only in the matters ejected from the stomach and bowels.

By this hypothesis he could explain all the obscure mysteries of Asiatic Cholera, whose symptoms were so contrary to every other systematic infective disease. This idea of the cholera virus not being absorbed into the blood was, so far as my father knew, quite original though he does not deny the possibility of its previous promulgation by someone else. It was quite new at any rate to many eminent physicians of the period and staggered more than Professor Syme. He himself says, 'The inference (non-absorption) seems strangely and unaccountably to have been totally overlooked by medical authors'.

With regard to treatment, it had been the custom to inject water into the veins in desperate cases only and for very different reasons than diluting the inspissated blood and making it flow. But the pamphlet shows that this should be the normal course of dealing with this disease. The author gives also the rationale of this practice, viz: to supply the blood with fluid from which the diarrhoea had removed the natural serum. Well did the old Romans say, 'Happy is he who knows the causes of things.' Now in one way or another, this method is invariably carried out.

There is one other point to which reference should be made. If, says he, the true cause of cholera be a fungus in the alimentary canal, why not attack the *fons et origo* of the mischief as well as injecting fluid into the veins which, after all, is merely palliative. What indeed he longed for was a direct antidote, 'mild as sulphur', that would not injure the mucous membrane nor poison the general system but yet be thoroughly effective in killing the fungi. Nature would do the rest. He was to learn more about this method in other diseases than cholera as the years passed, and so far as I can learn the idea was his own.

# 10

# MISCELLANEOUS ANECDOTES AND GHOSTLY INCIDENTS

One of the most moving cases remembered by my father was the case of Lady X. His practice by this time included some of the nobility and gentry, and at their homes he was in the way of meeting the physicians and surgeons from the teaching centres, and many an enjoyable crack had he with these superior minds, but he never obtruded himself, in fact he erred on the other side; he was too modest and unassuming.

In the castle of a titled family a maternity case turned up which gave him a deal of anxiety, so much so indeed that he at once informed the Baronet of the serious condition of his lady. The Baronet proposed an immediate consultation with Sir James Young Simpson and Dr. Ziegler, the two best obstetricians of the period. Next day the three met and all entirely agreed on the diagnosis, but differed altogether with respect to treatment. The two consultants were insistent, an operation without delay was the only chance, albeit a feeble one, of saving the patient.

This would have ended the matter in the majority of cases, the usual custom being to put aside one's own opinion and to accept meekly the *fiat* of the great consultants. So the latter were thunderstruck when Pairman boldly asserted that, in his humble opinion, an operation would almost certainly end fatally and proposed some less heroic measures. This completely staggered Sir James and Dr. Ziegler and they never forgot it, but neither consultants nor medical attendant yielded one point and they came to a deadlock.

## Miscellaneous Anecdotes and Ghostly Incidents

At the suggestion of the Baronet, the lady herself was consulted. She was very calm, listened patiently, and said something like this: 'Well, gentlemen, there are two against one, but these two cannot guarantee the success of an operation and yet they maintain that I cannot live without it. Dr. Pairman on the other hand, denies this, and is also against operating but thinks he can treat me with some prospect of success by a method not approved by the consultants. The question is a difficult one, but I am in God's hands and I decide in trusting Dr. Pairman'.

Soon all the gentry were familiar with the facts and these drifted down through the farmers to the workers and put the whole community into a state of keen expectancy. A few months passed, when the tension was at last relieved by the announcement that Lady X was delivered by Dr. Pairman safe and well.

So the country surgeon was right after all, and his reputation in the community established for all time. The last time Simpson and my father met was in Princes Street, Edinburgh, about 1870, when the illustrious Baronet got down from his carriage and shaking him heartily by the hand, said, 'Pairman, I have written a new book and have mentioned your name in it'.

The next incident is described by my father as 'A Fight for Life'. The morning of January 23rd 1868 was ushered in by a cloudless calm. The weather-diviners prognosticated a day of serenity, what is known locally as a 'Pet Day', a fragment of Summer faceted into the cold heart of a comfortless winter. But alas for the soothsayers! The forenoon had scarcely passed when a terrific tornado of wind and snow came shrieking along, tirlin' the kirks with a vengeance and bringing with it disaster and dismay. In the School darkness was so deep we pupils were summarily dismissed and on the way home were tossed like feathers in the storm. One boy was lifted, thrown against Christison's dyke, and knocked silly.

# A Scottish Country Doctor

My father had been visiting Scotston and was returning when he encountered the tempest in all its fury. It was all Ginger could do to make progress what with a solid wind and huge snowdrifts opposing it. The fences soon disappeared. It took an hour to cover less than a mile. When in the neighbourhood of Harestanes the doctor's hat blew off. He jumped out of the gig and ran after it but of course never reached it. When he turned round he could discover Ginger nowhere.

At length he got a glimpse of her, a considerable distance away, padding bravely through the snow. After a long chase he managed to catch up and, breathless and completely exhausted, he scrambled into the gig, and seized the reins. But he had only boards covered deep in snow to sit on, for the malicious wind had carried away everything moveable: whip, cushions, mat, apron, instruments and rug.

The poor doctor was in a pitiably sad case, almost *in extremis*. At long last he reached Mount Bog where lived Baillie the Roadman, who came to his rescue and helping, almost carrying him inside the cottage, supplied him with restoratives and comforted him with warm soup. Then rigging him up in old corn sacks and a big sou'-wester hat, Baillie drove him home, choosing the Broughton Road instead of by Skirling as being a shade more sheltered. A policeman at Broughton stopped him and hitched up a trace, trailing on the ground. And yet malignant people say that a policeman is never near when he is wanted!

But poor old patient Ginger! Fancy dragging a gig that long strenuous distance with only one trace. No wonder the doctor and his family idolised her!

I have told this story for several reasons: 1. It was the roughest storm the doctor had ever experienced, altho' he had encountered many. 2. Within a few months everything he had lost was restored, shewing the honesty and integrity of the people. 3. On this occasion he discovered how much less able he was to battle with the elements, which he had been accustomed to treat with indifference. 4. Because I wish to

introduce to you a man called Gavin Cree, a vanman employed by John Graham the Baker to deliver his loaves
around the countryside.

On this terrible Friday he too was out as usual, and when
the wind and snow became irresistible he somehow found a
more bieldy spot behind a high hedge, tethered his horse and
ensconced himself among the hot loaves inside the van.

When the doctor and Baillie reached the locality they could
perceive nothing but a huge wreath of snow moulded into an
uncommon shape, to which a horse was apparently linked.
But thinking a human tragedy had occurred, they made a
closer investigation, and were surprised to hear a 'god in the
car' shouting out in the true vernacular, 'I've taen nae skaith,
doctor. Juist let me bide and dinna fash!' Good old Gavin!

The next incident is a ghostly one, and bears witness to the
doctor's imperturbability. Every now and again a so-called
'ghost' would appear in the district, scaring the timid out of
their wits and sending the women and children home shrieking with terror. Even strong men succumbed to the power of
this ethereal visitant.

The Rev. Isaac Barrett of Skirling encountered it one night.
The ghost was jumping high into the air and capering about
to the utter undoing of the Irish gentleman who lashed his
adipose horse into a gallop-*ventre à terre* – and had a
gruesome and anomalous tale to recite on the following
morning.

A brother medico, usually with nerves of steel, fell under
the ghost's malign influence and reached home as pale as his
disembodied companion. He afterwards carried a revolver.

My own father was not to escape attention. Obeying a
night call, he went to the stable to saddle Ginger. While he
was so engaged he happened to turn his head and saw
standing in the doorway, grimacing like a demon, no less
a party than His Majesty, the Ghost himself. His cadaverous
semi-translucent countenance was certainly terrifying and it
is needless to deny that the doctor's blood, for a moment,

reversed its flow, but he controlled himself sufficiently to take no notice until the horse was fully equipped. He then blew out his lantern, and seizing a long hay-fork levelled its two deadly prongs at the ghost, at the same time leading the astonished Ginger by the other hand. Then he addressed the figure:

Whether you are in the body or in the spirit I intend to lead out my horse by that door. In front of me I hold a deadly weapon which I will not hesitate to use if need be. If you are a spirit two stabs will not hurt you. If you have a body, then God help you.

The Ghost withdrew!

Now we have another strange story, and explain it who can. It was a beautiful, calm moonlight night and the doctor was returning from Elsrickle when suddenly his horse became greatly terrified, snorted as is the manner of equines, and refused absolutely to proceed. Something which it perceived at the root of the hedge on the right hand was invisible to its rider. Whip and spur had merely the effect of making it rear and tremble all the more. Besides, Ginger was an intelligent beast and quite as sensible as Balaam's Ass, which appreciated the unseen better than Balaam himself.

They had reached the stone wall on the left, which supports the Churchyard ground. In this wall was a drainage slit, big enough to admit at a pinch a medium-sized dog, but too narrow and low to accommodate a man, let us say in ordinary circumstances. After a stiff tussle which lasted a considerable time, the doctor dismounted and led his horse past what was intimidating it, the animal all the while hugging the stone wall away from the hedge.

The doctor made a keen scrutiny of the source of fear and was at last horrified to see the figure of a man squatting by the roadside and partly hidden by the hedge. He was extremely emaciated and wore an expression of such devilish malignity that the doctor said that he could never have conceived such a malevolent aspect on any human face.

He spoke to the man but got no reply, so after stabling his horse he provided himself with a stout cudgel and went back for further investigation and to render any assistance he could. The vagrant was not to be found. The police were informed, who instructed all neighbouring villages to make inquiries and to keep a sharp look-out and report, but it was of no avail. The man had disappeared.

The question now is, had he insinuated himself into the hole in the wall or was this a case of spectral illusion where the mental eye sees clearer than the physical eye, such as Sir John Herschel and Sir David Brewster describe? Or could he be a real spiritual entity in corporeal form or one escaped from the tomb, anticipating the Resurrection, and taking 'a bit daunder by himsel'?

My father used to ask, if it were a mere subjective sensation, did the horse appreciate the apparition equally with its rider? If so, was this knowledge direct or communicated by the rider? A horseman certainly can unconsciously impart some of his feelings to his horse when in actual contact, but never through a loose rein, with the horse riderless. The doctor was convinced to the end that the figure was that of a man of material subsistence but he admitted the possibility of an illusion. Ginger's opinion was never obtained!

Another incident referred to by my father as 'A Riddle of the Night', is also impossible to explain.

On the Edmonstone Road in a cold biting Autumn wind, the doctor was trotting gaily along one night when his horse – not Ginger – shied badly at something it detected on the roadside, nearly throwing its rider. The latter got a glimpse of a man lying on his back and he stopped to investigate. At that moment a well-appointed carriage, all lights burning, with uniformed coachman and footman, came whirling round the corner.

My father arrested the vehicle and requested the footman

to bring out one of his carriage lamps that he might make his diagnosis. A gentleman passenger also jumped out and offered his assistance, stating that he was a London physician.

The two medicos examined the case together and agreed that the man was seriously ill, almost to the point of death, and it was resolved to convey the patient to the nearest cottage, some two miles away. With this intention they placed him in the carriage beside the physician, and the country doctor trotted home without further misadventure.

Some twenty years had come and gone and the incident had been almost forgotten, when he received an invitation to dinner from one of the upper ten who wrote, 'A gentleman from London has been reading your new book and greatly desires to meet you'.

He accepted and the two professionals passed an agreeable time together. They adjourned to the smoking room and my father casually inquired whether the visitor had ever been in the district before. The physician gave a curious laugh and said haltingly, as if he were brooding over something else, 'Yes . . . once . . . and I have . . . good reason . . . to remember my visit. I arrived at night and on the way from the station I encountered a country surgeon, bending over a dying man. We consulted together . . . and I agreed . . . to drive him to the nearest house'.

'Well,' exclaimed my father, 'this is extraordinary! I am the surgeon and I have often wondered how you got on. I have never heard of nor seen the man since I saw him with you on the roadside.' The physician was distressed and answered, almost in a whisper, 'Neither have I'. On being pressed, he continued, 'When we were both in the carriage, the patient became gradually worse and worse. The death-rattle was distinctly heard in his throat, his breathing became more and more shallow, more and more inaudible and intermittent till it finally ceased. Soon after, a cottage was reached and the carriage was stopped. I remained inside till the footman brought his lamp and opened the door. We carefully examined the carriage, the other door was shut, but – here comes the marvel – the carriage was EMPTY!'

Finally one more anecdote involving the mysterious and occult. One early morning the doctor awakened his wife to tell her of a disturbed dream which he had just had. 'I dreamt that yesterday afternoon I had extracted a tooth for John Girdwood and could not stop the bleeding. I was at my wits' end and awoke in a tremble.'

This story was no sooner told than a loud urgent knocking made the rafters ring. On opening the door he was astounded at the message, 'Johnie Girdwood is bluidin' tae daeth. Kelly pu'd a tuith for him yestreen and the bluid's never stoppit sin syne and Kelly's awa frae hame'. The doctor found the man blanched and pulseless but managed to effectively plug the socket. The human mind is certainly a tensile entity and can look before as well as behind! Such experiences gave rise to most interesting metaphysical discussions in the little parlour, when a learned and speculative company were gathered there, but could never be fully explained or understood.

# 11

## CHATS BY THE INGLENOOK

Brilliant discussions of a varied nature often took place in the parlour, when educated men – chiefly ministers – paid a social visit of an evening. I was too young fully to appreciate these conversations but I recollect many of the topics under review and the big words and phrases employed, sometimes with great emphasis: 'Erastianism', 'The Burgess Oath', 'The Original Secession', 'The Coming out of the Free Kirk', which aroused complacent but passionate enthusiasm, 'Catastrophism, and Uniformitarianism' of which I lapped up some precious drops, the 'Tractarian Movement' which reddened their faces and roused their combative instincts, 'Mere Popery'!

Little dogs have long ears and perchance longer memories, and I remember hearing about a man who 'felt Hell' burning in his own bosom. That was terrible! Why didn't he jump into the Milldam?

And there was Galileo who muttered between his teeth 'e pur si muove' although he had just sworn that it did not. But what moved or stood still was never quite apparent.

Then there was a chap called Bruno who was burned alive for saying 'In Nature are the thoughts of God'. Mr. Bruno should have held his tongue till he was able to prove it. And Luther who fell foul of the Calvinists for not approving of the 'Rising of the Peasants', and **John Knox** who tried to fly out of a pulpit but who 'never feared the face of Man' and 'trembled at nothing', surely a queer combination of temerity and folly.

And so on in an interminable succession of points glowing

on a background of blackness and ignorance. There was something powerfully attractive and yet somewhat terrifying in all this, especially when the discussions led to mysticism and metaphysical conundrums. To say that nothing really existed, or as they would now say 'subsisted', was to us a poser.

But it was when **Darwin** and his Theory were under review that my senses and perception became superlatively acute. I was born in January 1859, and in November of the same year was published *The Origin of Species*, a book that shook the world to its foundations. The treatises following its publication, written by **Huxley, Spencer, Tyndall** and others, accelerated the commotion.

So it is clear that I was cradled in an environment of evolutionary agitation and argument with repercussions all around. So impressed were we with the idea that we held with the monkey a common ancestry that we often visited the mirror and made faces to determine whether or not we could discover any simian feature. This we never could do in our own visage but had a strong suspicion about what we saw in the faces of our brothers and sisters!

Then there was the horrible suggestive fact that some of us inherited our grandfather's ability to move the skin of our scalp and to waggle our ears. The case however was judged 'Not Proven' but we felt inclined to add 'with a strong recommendation to mercy'!

Our Mother's verdict was 'I wudna wonder! I've seen, ma ain sel', some folk mair like gorillas than men but it's an awfu' thocht'. Yet I do not believe she was considering the question scientifically. When we were alone *en famille* she often lapsed into pure Doric, but when necessity called she could speak 'High English' as well as the best of them! None better!

What father actually thought about Darwinism and the recent pronouncements I cannot exactly tell. He had a very open mind to receive new theories if they were supported by logical evidence and did not trespass on the deductive position of God's written word. Few at that time knew enough about biological science, microscopic and otherwise, to pass an opinion of any real value. Although he did not deny the possibility of the truth of Evolution, he could not at once forego the interpretation of Genesis to which he had been accustomed. To his way of thinking the Bible could not essentially be wrong, so the argument resolved itself into this – either Science was not justified in drawing the conclusions it did, or we were misinterpreting the Bible. There must be a way out.

The new ideas did not disturb him personally, however, and he was quite content to await events, being fully cognisant of the fact that we were to draw, from the Book of Books, things new as well as old. The fact is that his mind was cast in such a metaphysical and philosophic mould and he had trained himself so to wander in these ethereal realms, that he could not be quite *en rapport* with the scientist's point of view.

It would seem that at the best he was rather inclined to agree with **Carlyle** and pronounce Darwinism a 'Theory of Dirt'. Why all this pother about gross matter, temporal in its very essence, when one could walk spiritually with the eternal, amid the glowing mountains of the invisible world!

I do not think Darwin's book was permanently in the house, nor indeed were the writings of Spencer, Tyndall and Huxley, but Father was perfectly familiar with them all, being always a discursive and voluminous reader.

In regard to his children he considered their judgment not sufficiently matured to grapple with these great minds. Lyell's *Principles of Geology* certainly was on our bookshelves but we, even the eldest of us, were forbidden to read it till our brains were more solidified, enough to be able to weigh evidence. I recollect scanning the famous *Vestiges of Creation* and wondering in a vague sort of way what it all meant. Hugh Miller's *Testimony of the Rocks* and his *Footprints of the*

## Chats by the Inglenook

*Creator*, as well as Thomas Dick's *Christian Philosopher* and his *Philosophy of a Future State*, we were permitted to read and we enjoyed them immensely.

In those days men were too close to the birth of the new theories to view them perspectively, and speaking generally there was a great deal of biased argument with a tinge of frivolous reasoning to colour it. When others waxed heatedly against the theories, denouncing them as contrary to the revelation of Scripture, Father's face remained unruffled and confident and he would remark, 'Well, gentlemen, we must not judge in haste but wait for more evidence. God's word cannot be overcome!'

In a similar manner he contemplated metaphysical problems, most puzzling to the human understanding, with equanimity. He was always content to wait with patience for the light which he believed was destined to come sooner or later. Thus far at any rate he was an evolutionist, but yet everything was in the hand and control of the Almighty who may work by law, though sometimes too mysterious for Man to understand. Drinkwater has since epitomised in poetic form the general attitude of father's mind with respect to such questions:

> Lord, not for light in darkness do we pray,
> Not that the veil be lifted from our eyes,
> Nor that the slow ascension of our day
> Be otherwise.
> Not these, Oh Lord, we would not break the bars
> Thy Wisdom sets about us, we shall climb
> Unfettered to the secrets of the stars,
> In Thy good time.

About this time there was a gardener at Cambus Wallace named Macpherson who was a vehement and impetuous Roman Catholic and fond of inciting his Protestant neighbours to an acrimonious argument. He was certainly too weighty for the latter and in desperation they appealed to 'the doctor' for assistance, who, nothing loath, at once noted down a few questions and required Macpherson to answer them.

What was his surprise to receive a reply couched in quite an elegant and learned style and presenting an adept's power of parrying the rapier's point, an achievement not usually reckoned a gardener's accomplishment.

That a priest's handiwork was involved was unmistakable, and somewhat tardily Macpherson admitted having shown the paper to his confessor at Lanark. This led to a correspondence with the priest, and my father challenged him to a disputation on various topics, which was accepted.

I once read quite a voluminous dissertation on transubstantiation written by Robert Pairman, which unfortunately was stolen from me years ago. So far as I can remember the contents, the author was fond of leading his opponent's argument slowly along and basing his premises on the conclusion of a previous syllogism till, all unexpectedly, he reached a *reductio ad absurdum* and then merrily tossed the subject about as a cat might play with a mouse. The priest was John Black of Lanark, but who was entitled to wear the laurel in this assault-at-arms I know not. In any case, religious polemics generally bear little fruit and that not very nutritious.

Robert Pairman was not a vindictive, contentious man. On the other hand he was of a particularly placid temperament, but dearly loved a friendly tilt with his compeers and invariably met rancour with a sportive disarming riposte.

The landed gentry liked to have Dr Pairman for a guest at dinner, especially when they had visitors from the City. They were fond of their genial family doctor and rejoiced when he entered the lists of a debate at a social gathering, his remarks being a mixture of sober truth and comicality. Some of these Town visitors were inclined sometimes to belittle the country surgeon and to consider him a mere unpolished sawbones.

## Chats by the Inglenook

On one such occasion a presumptuous guest of this type boldly and sneeringly asserted that he had an utter contempt for the profession of Medicine, and he kept on repeating that there was 'no philosophy in it, no philosophy whatever' in a loud and aggressive tone. This word 'philosophy' was such a magnificent term that it seemed to obsess him altogether, just as the word 'Mesopotamia' obsesses old ladies.

But our doctor cared no more for such disparaging remarks than he did for the impotent meaningless wheeple o' a whaup.

The other guests regarded him, but perceived nothing on his countenance except a faint gleam of kindly amusement. They seemed expectant, however, and remained silent. At last the doctor said in his quiet characteristic tone, 'Would you be kind enough, sir, to give us a definition of the word philosophy? It is well before beginning a debate to clearly define the terms used'.

This was a real strategic move, for no man from the palmy days of Parmenides to the present hour has been competent adequately to define the word.

The poor fellow's attempt was ludicrous, contradictory, and grossly involved, and the company soon discovered the entanglement into which his opponent had led him. They openly laughed.

This made him angry and defiant, and he shouted irritably, 'Medicine is mere quackery! Dr. Pairman cannot name one disease for which he knows a remedy he can positively swear will effect a cure'.

The doctor replied, 'Oh nonsense, I'll guarantee to cure Scabies or what is called the Scotch Fiddle with Flowers of Sulphur, in the twinkling of an eye. Yes, and without calling in the aid of philosophy to mystify either the patient or the audience'. This caused great laughter.

'Perhaps, sir, you can tell us what medical men would do with philosophy supposing they had it? Have you forgot that medical practice is a Science, is an Art, and has long ceased to bother about questions as to the source of Existence or the conception of pure Being, which properly belong to speculative philosophy and to nothing else? Once upon a time men groped in darkness and Medicine then was all philosophy, but the pregnant ages have given birth to scientific facts capable of demonstration, and when you talk of Philosophy in Medicine you are encroaching somewhat on its dignity.

'Democritus long ago indeed made the speculation, by his philosophy, that all matter was composed of Atoms, but in course of time scientific Dalton proved it, which is far better. You flatter us therefore when you say there is no philosophy in Medicine – in fact our whole aim for ages has been to get rid of it. Philosophy indeed!'

There was silence for a time, till one guest called out, 'You have met your match this time, Mr. X', which induced a deal of table-thumping and suppressed merriment.

But it was not the local dignitaries only that sought to entertain him; he was always welcome at the tables of the Edinburgh medical savants. But the demands of his practice prevented him fraternising as often as he would have desired.

At these meetings he usually met some distinguished representative of European culture. At one breakfast given by Sir James Y. Simpson, he had the honour and gratification of being introduced to **Signor G. Ruffini**, the celebrated author of *Dottor Antonio*, a work written in English and whose literary merits brought it into great prominence at that time.

My father took an immense interest in the Italian 'Risorgimento' and followed closely the varying fortunes of the secret society 'Giovane Italia' in her gallant struggle for freedom and independence. Cavour, Mazzini, Garibaldi and a host of others were continually being criticised in our house. He was therefore delighted to discuss the situation with such a prominent bandito and refugee as Ruffini and came home enthused with his experience.

Ruffini, if I am not mistaken, became in happier time an elected member of the first Government of United Italy, and he translated into Italian his book *Dottor Antonio*, which was as much appreciated by his own countrymen as it was originally by the British people. The emoluments derived from the English edition were generously devoted to relieve the hardships of his fellow-exiles resident in Britain.

# 12

# DIET, EXERCISE AND FERMENTATION

I remember my father best as a sturdy, thick-set, weather-beaten man of medium height, clean shaved, wearing a top-hat, a black professional surtout and Wellington boots tucked under his trousers, active and jovial.

After the illness to which I am about to refer he grew a short grey beard and whiskers but no moustache. He looked older than his years. His countenance was kindly, contemplative and inviting trust. His eyes were blue, clear and steadfast, his nose partaking of the Grecian type and his high forehead at once arresting one's attention. I shall take the liberty of quoting his own words:

In the winter of 1866–67 I happened to have more than the usual amount of toil and mistiming incident to a Country Doctor's life. Long cold drives, frequent long fasts, encroachments on sleep, and irregularities of meals. On the approach of Spring, although only eight and forty years of age, I began to feel excessively weak, much shortness of breath on ascending hills and a great deal of oppression at the chest.

This load showed itself by constant breathlessness and frequent inclinations to take a deep fetch or sigh, with great difficulty in getting to the bottom of it. As Spring advanced these symptoms greatly increased so that I felt as if utterly done.

I used to tell my family at this time that either some serious disease was impending or I was getting prematurely old, my constitution breaking up, and that I must of necessity soon be out of harness altogether. Yet at this time my appetite kept good, even unusually keen, and my stomach (as I thought) in first rate working order.

By the middle of April there was added to these symptoms fluttering of the heart conjoined with intermitting and irregular pulse. This fluttering rapidly passed on to frequent attacks of violent throbbing or palpitation, with a feeling of great faintness and exhaustion during their continuance. For whole nights together I would toss about in bed unable to sleep till a far advanced hour in the morning, my heart throbbing away most uncomfortably.

He had his teeth attended to and wore for a short time plates with an awkward hinge which he soon discarded and substituted suction plates for which he paid 75 guineas. The usual price was double that amount but the dentist considered his profession and reduced the fee.

Attributing his symptoms to nervous exhaustion and bodily weakness, he took various tonics, reclined as much as possible on a sofa and limited his practice. But one day he undertook a near-hand Midwifery case, and though he had simply to wait and that only for three hours, incessant palpitation and utter exhaustion were the result. He came away with the conviction 'My obstetrical career is for ever closed. Never more shall I aid woman in her hour of trial or help a squalling baby into the world again!'

He later adds this note: 'Alas for the short-sightedness of morbid anticipations. In one short month I was at my old work again, not only conducting an instrumental case of the greatest difficulty but in Surgery too, chopping off a leg without a flutter'. But before this happy condition of things had arrived he had to pass through a very trying experience.

These unusual freaks and plungings of the heart naturally created not only surprise but considerable alarm and he seriously asked himself whether this was an organic disease or only functional. He knew that two of his near blood relations had died from heart disease, which showed of necessity a hereditary tendency. In this dilemma he proceeded to consult a 'High Priest of the profession', to wit **Dr. Warburton Begbie** of Edinburgh.

In reply to the question, organic or functional? the High Priest could only reply, 'Well, my dear sir, I hope it may be functional. The valves are all right at any rate. But really with such an imperfect manifestation of the stomach symptoms I dare not at present give you a more decided opinion. Go off at once for a change of scene, have regular sleep and regular meals, come back in a month and then I will tell you all about it'.

He found this counsel eminently wise and judicious but felt it was more cautious than satisfactory and realised that even the highest skill might qualify its judgment by a 'hankerin' swither' that virtually sent him back to his own resources. His reflections in the train home were such as these: 'This waiting for a month to get my problem solved is not agreeable. I will instantly adopt more walking exercise and watch the result. For, clear enough, if this disease be organic, why, I am a dead man at any rate! But if it is only functional, this constant resting and lolling upon sofas is certainly not the way to cure it'.

This was a very philosophic way of accepting the position, but quite in accordance with his usual habit of mind. That very night he was delighted to feel a pain in the stomach and his neighbours remarked that he was looking bilious so he put these symptoms down on the side of his ailment being functional and instantly set about a total revolution in the matter of diet and discarded his tonic. Soon after, he set off for **Moffat** where he had ample opportunities of watching his disease in all its phases. This was in the year 1867, and in January 1868 he engaged in the prolonged 'Fight for Life' with a hurricane of snow and wind, already related in these reminiscences.

## Diet, Exercise and Fermentation

In studying his debilitated condition, he noted the effect of walking exercise which at first was merely 'creeping along in the way of putting one leg after another', but he found that even this creeping along gradually improved the pulse inasmuch as it intermitted less. He was also gratified to find that it strengthened the pulse if feeble or slowed it down when beating too quickly. The question then presented itself, How does walking act? 'Principally it is clear by assisting digestion and shaking the food away from the stomach. Assisting digestion! Oh, then this stomach of mine, with all its good appetite, really needs assistance and what more effective mode of granting it than by giving it exceedingly little to do. Shaking the food away from the stomach may be good enough but what right, pray, has such a disturber of the peace to get there at all?'

He forthwith resolved greatly to curtail the quantities of his meals, to have them closer between, and if need be, to have two light suppers instead of one, to make up the deficiency.

The success of the change was immediate and complete. This is why he called this regime 'The Great Supper Cure'. Hitherto he thought that by carefully selecting the proper materials and ever stopping short of full satisfaction he was doing his stomach every justice. But he soon discovered that frequent scanty meals were of infinitely more importance, and though selecting proper materials was not to be neglected, it occupied altogether a secondary place in the treatment.

His discovery of the signification of the erratic pulse was a source of great satisfaction to him, and even after his return to Biggar he continued his experiments and loved to show intelligent people how he could induce an attack of irregularity and how easily he could tranquillise it again. It was comforting to him to know that the intermitting pulse meant not an exhausted heart but merely bad nerves, while the feeble fluttering pulse was no proof of weakness either but only a proof of obstructed motion.

# A Scottish Country Doctor

The language of the intermitting pulse was 'Get quit of Bile, quit of Urea, which are poisoning the Nervous System', while that of fluttering was 'Get rid of Flatulence or some other load that won't allow the heart free room to play'.

As a continuation of this subject Dr Pairman wrote a paper entitled 'A Voice on Health from the School of Experience by A Country Doctor'. This was written in the first place for his own amusement, to hand round to his friends, professional and otherwise, but afterwards it was modified and continued in response to a request from the editor of a popular journal, but it was never published. All the medical men who perused it were thoroughly interested and strongly recommended its publication in pamphlet form. Dr Warburton Begbie, at that time head of the profession in Scotland, wrote, 'The manuscript has now beguiled the tedium of a journey to Dunfermline and I write these lines to express my concurrence in the views and opinions you have adopted and so judiciously advocate'.

The contents of the manuscript seem in these enlightened days a degree commonplace and unimportant, but in 1867 the subject of diet was scarcely considered at all, and the general opinion among the people was that if a man ate and drank well, became full in the cheeks and of a ruddy countenance, and above all if he developed a pronounced embonpoint, he was in the very pink of robust health.

In the case of children the dietetic injunctions were extremely nebulous and showed a dearth of fixed principles in the construction of a child's diet. Paediatrics at that time were certainly not in the ascendant. If this were true of the profession, what could one expect from the people? I remember an extreme case, amusing if perhaps hardly worth recording. A young, raw, big-boned, red-haired Amazon had unfortunately 'loved not wisely but too well' with the inevitable result. The product was a well-proportioned Hercules, like most that are born on the wrong side of the blanket. The doctor visited the Mother next day and put the usual query: 'Has the baby taken the breast?' The answer would have flattened a modern nurse in her starched cap and embroideries or perhaps knocked her silly altogether: 'No, but he is Deevil ta eat Cheese!' But this same baby survived, ultimately became a soldier and fought throughout the Great War.

Patients occupying the higher circles often resented inquiries about what they ate and drank and scorned suggestions dictated by science and common sense. The medical attendant indeed had often an unpleasant time before the patients would consent to submit to a restricted regime. But Father returned from Moffat thoroughly imbued with the idea that he had at his command a weapon of tremendous power both in the treatment of dyspepsia and of a great variety of other ailments, more especially if he could trace a connection between them and the nervous system.

Some of his cures I remember were very remarkable such as chronic rheumatism and asthma, eczema and other skin affections, insomnia, lupus and so on. He collected all the chronic cases whose management had puzzled consultants and family doctors alike, and the vast majority of those he either cured outright or greatly ameliorated. His practice rapidly increased, necessitating the engagement of an assistant, and he was often called to cases far out of his own district such as Peebles, Moffat, Lanark, Douglas, Carlops and Ninemile Burn etc.

Patients too consulted him either personally at home or by letter – sometimes twenty or more a day – from practically all over the country. Professors and other medical dignitaries sought his advice and sent invalids in whom they were specially interested, to be under his immediate care. Without a doubt the next few years saw him on the pinnacle of his fame.

But his mind as ever was dwelling on the theme of the welfare and happiness of the people. He recognised that much of the misery and discontent rampant in the world was in a great measure due to improper feeding. He had already attempted to reform and rectify the squalid conditions under which multitudes existed. If now he could only induce the people to amend their ways of eating and drinking, he would be helping to usher in a new and happier era for all humanity.

Partly with this purpose in view and also to divulge the duplicity of patent medicine mongers and designing quacks, he penned these papers on diet in a light, frolicsome style to instigate general perusal. These remarks apply specially to the last of the series which he denominated 'Stone Broth or Could the Millennium be Ushered in by Pills?' He was making arrangements to publish these papers when his attention and efforts were suddenly switched on to quite a different subject. To understand the position it will be advisable to dip a little into history.

The reader will recall that we left the determination of the cause of Asiatic Cholera in a somewhat indefinite condition. Father had accepted the suggestion of Professor Schonbeen who tentatively ascribed the cause to vegetable effluvia or 'Fungi, as they are called'. The world was now on the eve of making a tremendous advance and attributing many diseases other than cholera to specific living organisms acting within the body.

This theory had long been in a doubtful, quiescent state, which led to various speculations by inquiring and far-seeing men in the profession. But it was only in the latter part of the nineteenth century that it was generally accepted. This was brought about by a closer study of that mysterious process called fermentation, and this study was greatly aided by the use of more perfect and refined lenses in the construction of the microscope.

This subject took the most prominent place in discussions by the learned in current speculations during my adolescent years, and I remember being set to scan old medical journals and to cut out all references to fermentation and allied subjects to aid Father in his studies.

## Diet, Exercise and Fermentation

There were two schools of thought. One declared that fermentation was merely decay of organic matters, these having the principle of disintegration within themselves, while the other maintained that something must be added from without to begin the process, and that it must be alive and capable of growth and reproduction.

From as far back as the cholera days the latter was Father's opinion, reasoning from theory alone. In 1812 **Appert** found that fermentation could be prevented by boiling, which apparently meant that the vital element was killed. In 1836 Cogniard-Latour rediscovered the yeast plant and held that this was the cause of the fermentation of yeast. **Pasteur**, Tyndall, Lister and others afterwards confirmed this and Lister, in days to come, considered that putrefaction was merely a variety of fermentation, and that there was no such thing as 'spontaneous generation' of life, though Bastian and a few diehards maintained the very reverse.

In 1848 Fuchs stated that he had found excessively minute living organisms in the bodies of animals that had died of blood-poisoning, and in 1850 other organisms were detected in animals dead from anthrax or splenic fever. Wherever these diseases occurred, the specific organisms were invariably present, but whether these so-called 'Germs' or 'Microbes' were the actual cause of the diseases in question or the result of them or again merely associated with them, say as catalytics, remained for a long time a moot point.

The first proof that the modern 'Germ Theory' was correct was obtained by inoculating a healthy animal with the Bacillus Anthracis, thereby causing an attack of splenic fever. Bacteriology then became a science by itself. Bacteria however had been discovered more than 200 years before this and their discovery is quite a romance.

A linen-draper named Antony van Leeuwenhoek of the City of Delft, Holland, passed his leisure hours in cutting and polishing lenses, a hobby that brought him more fame after he was dead than during his lifetime. He constructed a kind of rude microscope, the precursor however of our present elaborate and almost perfect instrument, by making use of single lenses of short focus, and with this crude toy he made some marvellous discoveries.

In 1668 he demonstrated and wrote the first accurate account of the red blood corpuscles and in 1680 he noted that yeast consisted of minute globular particles and thus laid the foundation for future and greater discoveries in fermentation. But what further interests us here is that he was also the first to see bacteria or animalculae as he called them.

These he detected in water, saliva and dental tartar and even suggested that they might be the cause of many diseases. He was supported at the time by two shrewd Dutch medical men but he, with his potent observations, was soon forgotten, leaving the path open for Pasteur and Lister to follow in his steps. Thus arose the Germ Theory of disease and the system of Antiseptic Surgery which have been, all the world over, now generally accepted. Leeuwenhoek was a member of that half-mystical race of fascinating people, who, in the dim twilight, bore the standard of science before the rest of the world was prepared to receive it.

# 13

# THE GREAT SULPHUR CURE

We now come to the year 1867, an important epoch in the annals of medicine as well as in the life of Robert Pairman. In this year **Clifford Allbutt** introduced to the profession the Short Clinical Thermometer, which registers to the fraction of a degree the amount of fever in a patient. Before this time a clumsy instrument was sometimes used, but medical men in general depended on the 'Learned Touch' (*Tactus eruditus*) and the sensitiveness to heat of their own hands, and many a careful and experienced doctor could tell the progress or decline of a fever by this method alone. By long practice, wonderfully delicate and efficient did their hand become, but nowadays the tendency is for medical men to improve the mechanical aids rather than patiently cultivate their own inherent powers. In this same year Lister published his first paper on Antiseptic Surgery.

It was a tranquillising thought that scientists had at last discovered the visible actual cause of many obscure diseases. It put an end to vague speculation and indefinite theorising and gave something substantial for brain and hand to work upon. But it is very remarkable that Man for untold ages felt sure that the origin of his maladies was something outside himself, something that had got into him or attacked him from without.

Prehistoric men trepanned each other's skulls to let out the malignant spirit that caused epilepsy, and in the East we still come across people 'possessed of the Devil', and this is the only diagnosis ever offered. Even we at home continue to speak of 'a stroke', 'an attack', 'an incomin', 'a seizure' and so on. And that divaricating eruption on the chest called 'Shingles', that creeping belt (*Herpes zoster*), is yet regarded by many as the marks of the Devil's fingers.

Patients in the Highlands of Scotland suffering from this nervous eruption feel the shame of it. Is it not evidence of an unlawful colloguin' with Satan? They are shunned by their more righteous neighbours. Needless to say, Father was engrossed with the discovery of germs, which he had dimly seen in theory, away back in the old cholera days of mystery and conjecture.

Does the indulgent reader remember Gavin Cree who, in January 1868, encountered the snow-tornado of 'the awfu' Friday', and snugly weathered the storm in a baker's van among the steaming hot loaves? This same Gavin was quite a character in the community and a great reader of books heterodox and bizarre. He belonged to a family of nurserymen who introduced a new method of pruning forest trees, and some of his relatives and forebears were long recognised as illustrious authorities on arboriculture.

Well, the year before the storm, that is to say in 1867, Gavin, who was familiar with Father's conceptions about diet and his daydreams of a coming happier age for humanity, sent a pamphlet to him with a request for an honest criticism. This booklet was composed by a certain **James Dewar, M.D.,** Kirkcaldy, and described some extraordinary cures by common sulphur, either in the form of fumes as an inhalant or applied as sulphurous acid in a fine spray or as a lotion.

The requested criticism assumed the shape of a free and easy letter to the Rev. John Christison and, to use the writer's own words, 'written in such a hurry that it never cost more trouble than writing an ordinary letter'. Christison's only objection was the allusion to himself, but this was ultimately brushed aside and he exclaimed, 'Oh then I would not alter a word or comma'.

Not only so, but he willingly consented to write a Preface for the pamphlet itself. But before actual publication, Father

## The Great Sulphur Cure

submitted the manuscript to **Dr. Halliday Douglas** of Chalmers' Hospital, Edinburgh, through his friend Dr. Warburton Begbie. The former wrote, 'Every thoughtful practitioner will thank you for the just and earnest character of your inquiry', and the latter, 'I am greatly interested, instructed and amused'. No learned critic complained of its flamboyant title-page nor the merry style of the writing itself. So, early in October 1867 the pamphlet was launched before the public. The author laid no claim to originality but strongly supported Dr. Dewar's essay 'like two stranger country doctors shaking hands together without the formality of an introduction'. Its title-page had certainly the appearance of being somewhat quackish. It read:

The Great Sulphur Cure
Brought to the Test and workings of the
New Curative Machine proposed for
Human Lungs and Windpipes by
Robert Pairman Surgeon. Biggar
with a Preface by the Rev. J. Christison A.M.
Minister of Biggar.

From the very beginning the little brochure was an unqualified success, passing through five editions in the short space of one month and calling forth appreciative notices from the highest authorities. Among these testimonies were letters from **Professor Lyon Playfair, Dr. Joseph Bell**, etc. Edinburgh; Professors Gairdner and Buchanan, etc., Glasgow; Sir William Fergusson and Professor Law, etc., London; Professor Gamgee, Manchester, etc., which were all most gratifying to the author. But if the pamphlet caused a stir in the treetops, the branches nearer the popular level were far from quiescent. In Edinburgh, but more especially in Glasgow, the excitement over the Great Sulphur Cure was very great. I recall Johnie Lauder who kept a modest emporium of toys in Biggar, and who always visited Glasgow for supplies shortly before

Christmas, returning from one trip full of pleasurable per-
turbation and fussy zealous importance. Hurrying from the
station, he passed his own home to tell Father how great was
the 'Tirrikee' over his new book in the great Western City.

'Man, folks are crackin' aboot naething else, the book-
shops are plaistered baith ootside and in wi' the pamphlet and
I tell ye it was juist graun' tae see **Robert Pairman. Surgeon.
Biggar**, lookin' at ye frae every corner. I gaed intae twae or
three shops and telt them I kent ye weel, that ye were ma ain
doctor at Biggar and my word did they no' glower at me and
wonder'! Poor enthusiastic Johnie with his comic jovial face
and country drawl! Who can be surprised that the spruce
mercantile men 'glowered' at him and wondered!

In Edinburgh, on the other hand, where the people consider
it unseemly to openly disclose their feelings, the effervescence
was not so pronounced, but the interest was none the less real
and emphatic.

The Theatre Royal, at that Christmastide, had put on a
pantomime presenting a clever burlesque of the celebrities
appearing then in the limelight. One spectacle represented a
country doctor, very like Father, armed with a spray-produ-
cer, attending to a lady patient. The case is in the pamphlet
under the heading 'Common Cold and Hoarseness' and lends
itself conveniently to an exaggerated pantomimic representa-
tion. My brother Robert was in the auditorium and could not
but admire the talented way in which the actors carried it off.
There was a continuous ripple of laughter during the whole
performance.

But what was happening in sleepy little Biggar itself? There
was a rampant furore for sulphur burning as one might
expect, and Father was run off his feet experimenting and
administering the popular panacea, but never forgetting to
inculcate his principles of diet which he considered more
important than the Sulphur Cure itself. With both combined,
he sometimes worked miracles.

The people themselves treated every ailment under the sun

with brimstone in one or more of its various forms. It was nothing unusual to enter a shop and find the place like an actual Tophet, the shopmen coughing and sneezing, not indeed from catarrh, but from its remedy! They went on the principle 'Ye canna get owre muckle o' a guid thing'.

It was then that Father realised the danger of popularising a great medical discovery, and in the 13th edition published in February 1868 he writes: 'That the pamphlet should have appeared in a popular form instead of the pages of a Medical Journal is probably a blunder giving rise, as it has done, to some popular effervescence and flooding the market with many trashy appliances which, in ignorant hands, are fitted to bring the whole system into discredit. With human nature as it is, such evils are almost necessary concomitants of every step in advance, which time alone can be expected to cure'.

In the last edition of the pamphlet – the 16th, I think – he changed the title to 'The Great Sulphur Cure or Sulphurous Acid in the Treatment of Disease', which the publishers stereotyped.

But Man was not the only subject for experiment. He tried sulphur and its compounds on dining vegetables in the kitchen garden. He taught the farmers' wives and dairymaids how to keep milk sweet in all weathers. He preserved fish, meat and other organic comestibles for weeks together and hastened the churning of milk in the manufacture of butter. He even fed sulphites to fowls and rabbits six or eight days before killing to prevent decomposition.

In association with Mr. Thorburn of Quothquan he wrote a paper on the effects of sulphurous acid on churning milk, which was presented to the Royal Society, Edinburgh, and the writers were advised to continue their investigations.

But what enthused him most was that at last, after years of dreaming, he became acquainted with a substance 'Mild as Sulphur itself' to attack disease germs multiplying in the body and to be treated by internal medication. Patients suffering from specific fevers, pneumonia, etc. were treated with remarkable and encouraging results. It may be of interest to relate two cases with which I was personally associated. The first may be called 'Spiders and Immortality'.

My cousin Robert of the Bank and I were boon companions in mischief and adventure. Our stable, whose ceiling, walls and window were festooned gloriously with spider webs, was our customary rendezvous. One day we resolved to get rid of the spiders at one fell swoop. Robert proposed sulphur fumes. Both horses were out so we did not spare the sulphur. Soon the apartment was suffocating. Just then Father arrived with Ginger, reckoned the house was on fire, and demanded an explanation. Meekly it was given. 'Kill the spiders, you silly gowks! You are more likely to render them immortal by killing their foes the deadly germs. What put such a ridiculous idea into your heads?'

In a grumbling and offended tone I answered, 'Well, you said yourself that the same poison that destroys a wasp is very likely to kill a flea, and we thought it would do the same to spiders!' At this problematical argument the doctor took a very hearty laugh and dismissed the delinquents with a caution.

The second case had a happier ending. Maggie had received from a friend the gift of a singing bird, a beautiful canary whose plumage everybody admired. But it was a pathetic little figure, much addicted to noiseless yawning, and, although it belonged to a musical species, it was never known to give a cheep, much less to warble. It might have been a Trappist monk for all we heard to the contrary.

We spoke to it, whistled to it, played the piano, rattled tea-cups and tin-cans, but for three years it remained positively dumb. It only yawned and twisted its head. But we never know our future.

Unknown and unexpected by us all, deliverance was at hand. I had lit, for some legitimate purpose, a little brimstone in the parlour where Dickie's cage always hung.

To the surprise of everybody, and doubtless of itself, it

suddenly, Caedmon-like, burst into a veritable rhapsody of song, deafening but melodious. Who can decry the Great Sulphur Cure after that?

It would have been strange had the Press not shared in the public discussion, and many newspapers admitted various writers to its correspondence column. The *Glasgow Herald* printed leading articles entirely in its favour, which called forth many letters for and against the Sulphur System. Maggie at that time acted as her Father's private secretary and kept all letters and newspaper cuttings, most of which have been lost or destroyed.

Father answered only one letter which was written anonymously by a medical man who turned out to be Donald Campbell Black, M.D., Glasgow. Only this one letter in reply has resisted time and accident. It reminds me of the speeches delivered by astute barristers in the Criminal Supreme Court to which I was long compelled to listen.

The upshot of Campbell Black's criticism, which was initially hostile, was however an admission of his error, and he came to Biggar and saw the country surgeon at his work and ultimately became an enthusiastic advocate for the Sulphur System.

# 14

## APPROACHING THE LAST LAP

After the 'Fight for Life' in the snowstorm of 1868, Father continued his ever-increasing practice. Among his patients were many wealthy Glasgow merchants who pled with him to leave Biggar and settle in the Western Metropolis. I remember the inducement offered: 'The Golden Ball is at your feet and you have only to pick it up to realise a fortune'. But they did not know their man. What was gold to a mind of his quality? He had other bread to eat of which they knew nothing. He was so attached to Biggar and his trusting patients that he had not the heart even to consider leaving them. And to give the latter their due, they fully appreciated him as he deserved.

One Sunday night my father told the family circle that there were two things he most earnestly desired and prayed for. First, that he would die away from home, and second, that he would die suddenly. Both of these petitions were answered.

About this time the University of Edinburgh proposed conferring on him the degree of M.D. *honoris causa*, but he never gave the messenger a decided answer. It did not appeal to him.

In the late summer of 1871 he was being driven to the Railway Station in a public conveyance belonging to one of the hotels, when, through careless harnessing, the blinkers of the horse fell off. The animal took fright and set off at full gallop down the street. Father was described to me as having lost his hat and sitting as pale as death, awaiting the inevitable.

Through long custom, the horse negotiated the various turns of the road and crossed with safety the Neilsen Bridge, across the burn. But when the station was reached, the carriage collided with the stone building and overturned on its two occupants, the horse meanwhile lying on its side kicking furiously.

The onlookers expected to witness a fatal tragedy. Father's consciousness was the first to return, and he found himself among the wreckage, in dangerous proximity to the horse's heels. He disengaged himself, and wriggled out on his hands and side thinking 'I am alive at any rate'. He went at once to help in restoring the driver who was still *hors de combat* and insensible.

When I came into the Parlour, boisterously calling for my eleven o'clock 'piece', I found Mother tenderly bending over Father who was seated in his accustomed armchair. He was very pale and very calm and I detected in his eye a faint but quite discernible squint, a bruised and swollen temple, and torn trousers.

In the afternoon the doctor insisted on visiting the coachman, whose dwelling was nearby, but this short journey proved too much for him and he had to take to bed where he remained for a week or so, with Drs. Alexander and John Kello in attendance. He was not bled as on the occasion of his broken thigh, which caused a merry discussion among the three medicos.

Father was never the same again. Writing now with an experience of severe accidents, during many years in a seaport town, I reckon this casualty induced two results, which became more apparent as time went on. The first was aortic regurgitation and the second was a permanent injury to the brain. Aortic regurgitation itself disturbs the nicely balanced cerebral circulation and often causes mental trouble. All the more so, however, when a lesion already exists in the brain, indicated by squint etc.

Father's accident included certainly a prolonged mental strain and struggle before the final catastrophe, whose effect at first sight was only a slight lesion of the brain, indicated then by a slight squint. The cardiac symptoms appeared later.

But he recovered so far as to resume practice, and in 1872 he wrote and had printed a short paper to distribute among the people on the benefits of revaccination. An epidemic of smallpox was prevailing in the neighbouring cities. The folder found its way into the hands of many medical men and was well commented on, especially by Professor Gairdner of Glasgow and by Dr. Russell, physician of the Glasgow Smallpox Hospital. This is what the latter wrote:

> May 10th 1872. It is a clear, concise, plain and convincing statement of the case for revaccination. I am quite delighted with it, and only wish it were more common for medical men to seize hold of a fact with such an unwavering grasp, and go before the public with their opinions on a point of much practical importance, equally firm and absolute.

Dr. John Brown and Professor Alexander Simpson considered that the tract should be published in pamphlet form and strongly recommended Father – in fact urged him – to write a series of pamphlets on subjects interesting to the profession. After due consideration he resolved to accede to their request. This work was begun but not continued, as the reader will shortly understand. The series was to be called

Quackery in General & Antiseptic Medicine in Particular.
A Series of Tracts chiefly addressed to the
Medical Profession.
No. 1 – Smallpox and its Antidote or The Pioneer.

The next of the series was to be on Diet, including ultimately 'Stone Broth or Could the Millennium be ushered in by pills?'

Before leaving the subject of 'Smallpox and its Antidote', I should like to say that this little tract written first for private circulation but afterwards reproduced in a more permanent form, caused a stampede to our house. All wished to be vaccinated, and for several days the parlour was filled to overflowing with humanity of all ages. Robert, my cousin, was sent over and entered the room blushing and wriggling as boys often do.

He was astonished to see so many women and girls with naked arms and shoulders (females were not so prodigal of their charms as they are nowadays) and the blush took a deeper tint on his 13-year-old cheeks. Father took in the whole position in a flash, and his native fun and humour could not be suppressed. Addressing the boy solemnly and professionally, he said, 'So you wish to be vaccinated, Robert. Very well, just take down your trousers!' An over-sensitive flapper suppressed a kind of shriek and titter which set the whole room into convulsions of laughter!

By the winter of 1871–72 father was feeling more and more the hardships of his far-flung country practice and we often heard his yearning for a little more peace and quiet and time to pursue his literary bent. Climbing hills was his greatest difficulty. One day he was struggling up a trackless height to visit a patient when he met a robust brawny shepherd and said to him, 'Sandy, do you ever lose breath going up this hill?' The question surprised the herd and he answered querulously 'Ay if I rin a' ma pith!' The reply tickled the doctor and he often told the anecdote with laughter.

Here and onwards I am uncertain as to exact dates. But I recollect one occasion when he and his groom were out driving and Father had to visit a house on the top of a little incline, a short distance from the road. William was watching and perceived that he was in great distress and hurried to his assistance. When they reached home, William helped him into the kitchen where Mother and some of us were standing. He looked exhausted, pale and breathless and said in a calm and resigned tone, 'Ah, Margaret, but for William here I never could have reached home', and then he added pathetically, 'The pitcher goes many times to the fountain but it comes home broken at last, and that, I am sure, is my case'.

The aortic trouble was declaring itself more emphatically. Mother had often pleaded with him to retire from practice and live where he could study and write without disturbance. But now she insisted upon it. This he soon practically did.

Ginger was pensioned off on the farm of Mr. Gibson, Persilands, to be used sparingly but never to be sold, and he introduced the Doctors Kello to his best patients. This must have been in the Autumn of 1872, so far as I can judge. He now passed his time in study and in walking exercise, especially down John's Loan and by the burnside, and I often accompanied him. We observed at this time that his memory was failing and that sometimes he had a difficulty in exercising his judgement and got entangled in his phrases, much to our distress and to his own also.

He was always kind and thoughtful, however, to those around him, ever prone to crack a joke with any one we chanced to meet and ever ready to help and to commend a generous deed. In this condition he was anxious to go to Edinburgh for a time, and although his family doubted the wisdom of allowing him to go alone, they at last permitted him to proceed.

Of course he had many friends in the City in whose homes he was always a welcome guest. Maggie went to the station with him. Observing her much upset and crying, he patted her kindly on the shoulder and, having kissed her, said, in a soft paternal tone, 'Cheer up, Maggie, the present seemeth not joyous but grievous, nevertheless afterwards it yieldeth the peaceable fruits of righteousness'.

Whether he consulted a physician about his condition I cannot say, but he did not stay long in the City. Moffat had done him good before, so to Moffat he returned and Mother joined him there. She called in two brain specialists from Dumfries who declared the heart to be incurable but strongly recommended his living in a home specially adapted for such cases. They noted the squint had become more apparent and thought they might succeed in removing the cause but nothing definite was promised.

The three drove away together. He improved very considerably under their constant care and treatment but the heart remained unchanged and troublesome, as they had expected. He passed a very happy quiet time at Dumfries. The doctors frequently called on him to assist in the diagnosis of obscure cases occurring in the neighbourhood, and they quite enjoyed his company and were struck with the acumen he displayed in suggesting points to look for, and in the treatment by his diet principles.

The family in Biggar was not forgotten. Mother received an occasional letter written in his usual humorous and affectionate strain and containing a message to each of us, named in order. We were all hoping to see him again restored to health, but this was not in God's plan. The Sabbath morning of February 9th, 1873, broke cold and uninviting. He sought a cosy room and, reclining on a soft low couch, drawn up before a roaring fire, he lit his pipe and enjoyed reading the large-typed Bible which we had sent to him at his request.

He had passed a somewhat painful restless night but now he was more comfortable. Holding the Bible in his left hand, he with his right made use of the stem of his pipe to assist him in following the words and lines. This he often did in former days, taking a few puffs occasionally. In this position his spirit took its flight to the Better Land:

> Night slipped to Dawn and Pain merged into Beauty,
>    Bright grew the road his weary feet had trod;
>       He gave his salutation to the Morning,
>    And found himself before the face of God!

His body was brought to Biggar one dark night and lay, till the day of interment, in the Little Parlour, a room now doubly sacred to the family. Next morning we were all brought in to look upon his familiar, placid face for the last time. Of course under these melancholy conditions human nature could not be controlled, and there were some convulsive sobs and a little quiet weeping. But what did we really see through our tears? Speaking for myself, I, 'wee Socrates', and the humble writer of these imperfect reminiscences, saw, not so very far away either, shining in a Living Light a beautiful Gate of Pearl. How true is George Gilfillan's dictum: 'The most powerful of all telescopes is a tear'!

Thos. Wyld Pairman.
January 20th 1934.
Governors Bay, New Zealand.

# HISTORICAL AND BIOGRAPHICAL NOTES

(Subjects indicated in bold type on the relevant page of the text)

## Chapter 1

p.5 **Mitchelhill** was later the home of James Watson and his wife Jeanie, the daughter of Sarah (Galbraith) Wilson. Their daughter Jessie was born at Mitchelhill in 1856, and later married Dr. Pairman's son Robert, who would be the grandson of Rachel Davidson who had lived there 70 years before.

p.7 **The French Prisoners.** Dr Pairman's wife Margaret was the daughter of Adam Wyld and his wife Margaret (née Cuthbertson) who had previously been married to one of these prisoners, Jean Pasquier de Blin, an officer in the French army. After the war she went with him to live in Paris, where they had a baby daughter who sadly died in infancy. Soon afterwards her husband also died and she came back to Biggar, bringing with her new styles and fashions which were welcomed by the weaving community. She also brought a French cooking pot which is in the Gladstone Museum in Biggar.

## Chapter 2

p.10 **John Brown, 1810–1882**, physician and essayist, born at the Manse in Biggar, the son of the Rev Dr John Brown, and grandson of the Rev John Brown of Whitburn. Studied medicine at Edinburgh University. Best known as author of

*Rab and his Friends*, he also wrote *Pet Marjorie*, an essay on the child writer Margaret Fleming, *Horae Subsecivae* (Leisure Hours) and various other papers. He was a friend of Thackeray, Ruskin and Mark Twain.

p.12 **Robert Forsyth, 1766–1845**, born in Biggar, the son of Robert Forsyth, bellman and gravedigger and his wife Marion Pairman. He studied four years at Glasgow University and after graduating he attended the Divinity Hall in Edinburgh. He was licensed to preach while still only twenty years old, but lacking a patron, he eventually became a lawyer in 1792. Among his writings were several articles for *Encyclopedia Britannica*, *Principles of Moral Science* (1805), *A Life of Dr Johnson*, and *Beauties of Scotland* (1806). In his profession, many regarded him as the equal of Jeffrey, Cockburn, Murray, and Moncrieff, the leading lights of the Scottish Bar, but he was 'contented to be ranged with the ordinary class of champions' and probably lost work because of his support and defence of the Scottish political martyrs of that period.

p.14 **John Pairman, 1788–1843**, the doctor's uncle, was apprenticed to a draper in Glasgow, and later set up business in Biggar. After a few years he gave up the business to become a professional portrait painter, at first in Glasgow and later in Edinburgh. Many of his family portraits have been lost but the portrait of Nancy mentioned here is reproduced as plate 4. He was also the painter of the portraits of Robert reproduced as plate 1 and probably of the portraits reproduced as plates 2 and 3.

p.17 **Professor Johnstone.** The Johnstones and Browns were related and can trace their ancestry back to John Brown of Haddington, the theologian. A twentieth-century descendant is His Honour Judge Ian Graeme Mclean of Winchester, to whom we are grateful for providing various family details. (The Pairmans are also related – see family tree.)

p.18 **Thomas Chalmers, 1780–1847, theologian and preacher.** Born in Anstruther and educated at the University of St Andrews. Professor of Moral Philosophy at St Andrews, 1823–28, and Professor of Theology at Edinburgh until 1843 when he led a group of Scottish clerics to form a new organisation – the Free Church of Scotland. The Free Church founded a college in Edinburgh, and Chalmers became its first Principal.

# Historical and Biographical Notes

p.18 **Sir William Hamilton, 1788–1856.** Born in Glasgow, studied at Glasgow University and Balliol College, Oxford. Professor of Civil History at Edinburgh 1821–38, and Professor of Logic and Metaphysics 1838–56. An educational reformer, he deplored the high degree of illiteracy which was tolerated in England.

p.18 **Monro Tertius, 1776–1859,** followed his father and grandfather as Professor of Anatomy in Edinburgh. Alexander Monro (Monro Primus), 1697–1767, and his son Alexander Monro (Monro Secundus), 1733–1817, were both famous in their day, the latter specialising in the nervous system, particularly brain, ear and eye. Monro Tertius was not quite as distinguished as his two predecessors, but he was a very capable anatomist and teacher who trained at least eleven professors and countless doctors.

p.18 **Sir Robert Christison, 1797–1882.** Born at Kilmarnock. Toxicologist. Studied medicine at the Universities of Glasgow and Edinburgh. Professor of Medical Jurisprudence at Edinburgh 1822.

p.18 **James Syme, 1799–1870,** surgeon, born in Edinburgh. Considered one of the finest surgeons of his age. Studied under Robert Liston in Edinburgh, also in Paris and Germany. In 1818 he announced a method of waterproofing, patented by Charles Macintosh. In 1829 he established a private hospital in Edinburgh.

p.19 **Robert Liston, 1794–1847,** surgeon. Born at Ecclesmachan Manse, Linlithgow. Studied in Edinburgh and London. Became lecturer in surgery and anatomy in Edinburgh in 1818. In 1835 became Professor of Clinical Surgery at University College, London. He was the first to use general anaesthetic in a public operation at University College Hospital on December 21st 1846.

p.19 **John Lizars, c 1787–1860,** surgeon, son of Daniel Lizars, a publisher. Born in Edinburgh about 1787. Educated at Edinburgh High School and University. Fellow of the Royal College of Surgeons 1815, and appointed Professor of Surgery at the Royal College of Surgeons in Edinburgh in 1831, when he became senior operating surgeon at the Royal Infirmary. He introduced the operation for the removal of the upper jaw, and his name is remembered in the medical profession by the 'Lizar's Lines'.

p.19 **Minto House** was part of the old Edinburgh Royal Infirmary which was demolished in the 1870s. Minto House itself still exists and is now part of the University.

p.19 **Sir Charles Bell, 1774–1842**, anatomist and surgeon, particularly noted for his work on the brain and nervous system. He studied at Edinburgh University where he later became Professor of Surgery.

p.20 **Lord Lister – Joseph Lister, 1st Baron, 1827–1912.** Born at Upton, Essex and educated at the Universities of London and Edinburgh. In 1861 he was appointed surgeon at the Glasgow Royal Infirmary. His discovery of antiseptics in 1865 greatly reduced the number of deaths from operating-room infections. In 1897 Lister was made Baron by Queen Victoria, who had been his patient.

p.20 **Sir William Fergusson, 1808–1877**, son of James Fergusson of Lochmaben, Dumfriesshire. Educated at Edinburgh High School and University. Became Fellow of the Edinburgh College of Surgeons in 1829, and in 1831 was elected surgeon to the Edinburgh Royal Dispensary. In that year he tied the subclavian artery which had then been done in Scotland only twice. In 1840 he became Professor of Surgery at King's College, London. He was President of the Pathological Society in 1859–60 and of the British Medical Association in 1873. He died in 1877 and was buried with his wife at West Linton, Peeblesshire.

p.21 **Sir James Young Simpson, 1811–70.** He took his MD at Edinburgh in 1832 and became President of the Royal Medical Society in 1835 and Professor of Midwifery in 1839. He was famous for the introduction of chloroform in 1847. Created Baronet in 1866.

p.21 **Professor Thomson, 1773–1852.** Chemist born in Crieff, Perthshire. Studied at St Andrews and Edinburgh, graduating as a doctor in 1799. Editor, writer, historian. In 1817 held a Chair at Glasgow University. He was one of the first university lecturers to insist on systematic training in practical work.

p.21 **James Howe**, artist, was the subject of a biography by Sandy Cameron. His paintings are said to be racy and full of life, although 'primitive'.

# Historical and Biographical Notes

## Chapter 3

p.23 **Robert Knox, 1791–1862**. Anatomist, born in Edinburgh. He became Conservator of the newly established Museum of Edinburgh Royal College of Surgeons, and from 1826–40 ran the anatomy school. He won fame as an anatomist but aroused considerable dislike through having obtained subjects for dissection from Burke and Hare. He is the subject of James Bridie's play *The Anatomist*.

p.26 **Sir Douglas Maclagan, 1812–1900**. Fellow and President of the Royal College of Physicians and Surgeons at Edinburgh. He was the brother of the Most Rev William Dalrymple Maclagan, 1826–1910, Archbishop of York. Their father was Dr David Maclagan. We are told by Thomas Wyld Pairman that this Dr Maclagan once lived at The Stane near Biggar, which was previously the home of his Pairman ancestors.

## Chapter 4

p.28 **Professor Hope, 1766–1844**. Chemist. Thomas Charles Hope was born in Edinburgh and studied medicine at the University there. Taught chemistry at Glasgow and Edinburgh. Highly successful teacher – the first to teach the new ideas of Lavoisier – the Father of Modern Chemistry.

p.30 **Dr J Argyle Robertson**. President of the Royal College of Surgeons in Edinburgh, and father of Douglas Argyle Robertson, 1837–1909, who was Surgeon Oculist to Queen Victoria and King Edward VII in Scotland.

## Chapter 5

p.35 **Dr George Kello** was a second cousin of the Prime Minister W E Gladstone. Gladstone's father was Sir John Gladstone of Leith. There were several more distant cousins living in the Biggar area including Brian Lambie's mother Peggy Gladstone and the various Gladstones who were connected with the Pairman family.

## Chapter 6

p.45 **Margaret Cuthbertson Pairman** was the grandmother of Margaret Meiklejohn and of Sarah, John and Richard Miller, mentioned in the Introduction.

## Chapter 7

p.55 **Mr. John Buchan, Writer, Peebles,** was a solicitor who had set up his own law firm in Peebles in 1850. He was the grandfather of the famous author of the same name.

There are other family connections with John Buchan the author. When the Wilsons (Sarah Galbraith's family) left the old home at Burnetland in Broughton, it was bought by the author's uncle Ebenezer, mentioned in some of his writings as 'Uncle Eben'. The young John spent many happy holidays there. Broughton was also the home of his maternal grandfather John Masterton, and he always had a great affection for the area. His little sister Violet, who died in 1893 at the age of 5, is buried in Broughton Churchyard.

p.58 **Tinto Hill** is a well-known local landmark. At 2,350ft it is the highest point in Clydesdale, but is beaten by Coulter Fell (2456 ft), the summit of which is just into Peeblesshire.

## Chapter 8

p.66 **Dr Richard Mackenzie, 1821–1854.** Chief Assistant to Professor Robert Liston at Edinburgh Royal Infirmary. He volunteered to serve in the Crimean War and died of cholera at the age of 33. His position under Liston was taken by Lister, a Quaker who could not do war work.

## Historical and Biographical Notes

### Chapter 9

p.73 **Dr George Combe, 1788–1858.** Phrenologist, born in Edinburgh and attended the St Cuthbert's parish school and Edinburgh High School. Admitted as Writer to the Signet in 1812. In 1820, with David Welsh and others, he formed the Phrenological Society and started the *Phrenological Journal*. In 1824 he published *Elements of Phrenology*. In 1836 he was a candidate for the Chair of Logic at Edinburgh, but was outvoted by his old opponent Sir William Hamilton. During his latter years he was much occupied with the question of relations between religion and science.

### Chapter 11

p.86 **John Knox, c. 1513–1572.** Scottish religious reformer and founder of Presbyterianism in Scotland. Born in Haddington and educated at the University of Glasgow. He was originally a Roman Catholic priest but was influenced by the Protestant reformer George Wishart. In 1551 he was appointed Chaplain to Edward VI, but when Mary Tudor became Queen he fled to France, where he met the Protestant reformer John Calvin.

p.87 **Charles Robert Darwin, 1809–1882.** Born in Shrewsbury and educated at Shrewsbury School. His maternal grandfather was the china and pottery maker Josiah Wedgwood. He began to study medicine at Edinburgh University, but dropped out of medical school to study for the Church at Christ's College, Cambridge. He finally became a scientist and naturalist and is best known for his *Origin of Species*, published 1859, which caused great consternation, especially in religious circles.

p.87 **Thomas Henry Huxley, 1825–1895.** Biologist and active supporter of Darwin's theory of evolution. Graduated in medicine at the University of London (Charing Cross Hospital) and in 1845 became a member of the Royal College of Surgeons. He travelled widely and was made Fellow of the Royal Society in 1850.

p.87 **Herbert Spencer, 1820–1903.** Philosopher, journalist and writer on biology, psychology, sociology and ethics. His

*System of Synthetic Philosophy* explored various theories of evolution and the impact of Darwin's writings.

p.87 **John Tyndall, 1820–1893.** Physicist, born in Ireland. Studied at the University of Marburg in Germany. Professor of Natural Philosophy at the Royal Institution of Great Britain in 1854. He succeeded Michael Faraday as Superintendent in 1867. He studied chemistry with Robert Wilhelm Bunsen and in 1869 he disproved the theory of spontaneous generation.

p.88 **Thomas Carlyle, 1795–1881.** Scottish essayist and historian. Born in Ecclefechan and studied Divinity at the University of Edinburgh, but later turned to Mathematics and Law, and also German Literature. He wrote for the *Edinburgh Review* and was considered in the nineteenth century to be one of the leading thinkers of his age.

p.92 **Giovanni Dominico Ruffini, 1807–1881.** Born in Genoa, he became a member of Young Italy Republican Movement in 1833, when he fled to England. *Dottor Antonio*, one of his best known books, was written in 1855.

## Chapter 12

p.96 **Dr James Warburton Begbie, 1826–1876,** physician, second son of Dr James Begbie. Educated at Edinburgh Academy and the University of Edinburgh. He studied in Paris, specialising in diseases of the skin. In 1852 he settled in Edinburgh as a family practitioner and became a Fellow of the Royal College of Physicians. For the remainder of his life he was acknowledged as the most popular and highly esteemed physician in Scotland.

p.96 **Moffat.** The Pairmans seem to have had strong links with the town of Moffat, about 20 miles south of Biggar. At this time the town was a Spa and Dr Pairman went there on at least two occasions to recuperate after illness. Later his eldest daughter Margaret married John Miller, who had a draper's business in the town, and they lived there with their young family for many years, first at Rosebank and later in a larger house called Elmwood. When Dr Pairman died his widow went to live in Moffat, first at Lyne Bank and later at Park House, where she lived with her daughter Rachel until her death at the age of 80 in 1906.

## Historical and Biographical Notes

p.101 **Nicolas Francois Appert, 1749–1841.** French chef and confectioner. He opened the world's first commercial canning factory in 1812. In 1795 he began experiments with hermetically sealed containers in response to a call from the French government for a solution to the problem of feeding their expanding army and navy. He won a government prize of 12,000 francs for his method of using the autoclave for sterilisation.

p.101 **Louis Pasteur, 1822–1895.** French chemist and biologist who founded the science of microbiology. Proved the germ theory of disease. Invented the process of pasteurisation and developed vaccines for various diseases including rabies. He also did research on fermentation and the role of yeast.

## Chapter 13

p.103 **Clifford Allbutt, 1836–1925.** Physician and writer. He was the inventor of the short clinical thermometer.

p.104 **Sir James Dewar, 1842–1923.** Chemist and physicist. Born in Kincardine and studied at the University of Edinburgh. Became Professor of Experimental Natural Philosophy at Cambridge in 1875 and Professor of Chemistry at the Royal Institution in 1877. He invented the Dewar flask, the first vacuum flask.

p.105 **Dr Halliday Douglas**, a Fellow of the Royal College of Physicians in Edinburgh. He wrote *Statistical Report on the Edinburgh Epidemic Fever of 1843–1844*. In 1864 he was the first physician to be appointed to the Chalmers Hospital and in the same year he became President of the Royal College of Physicians of Edinburgh.

p.105 **Professor Lyon Playfair, 1819–1898, 1st Baron.** Scientist, born in India. Studied medicine at St Andrews, Glasgow and London. Manager of a textile printing works at Clitheroe in 1840. Professor of Chemistry at Edinburgh, 1858–68. Liberal MP from 1868. His main interests were in Public Health and Social Welfare. Introduced pensions for the aged poor. Postmaster General; Vice-President of the Council; Lord-in-Waiting to Queen Victoria. His brother William Smoult Playfair was obstetrician to the royal family.

p.105 **Dr Joseph Bell, 1770–1843.** George Joseph Bell, brother of Sir Charles Bell. Born in Edinburgh. Professor of Scottish Law at Edinburgh University

# Sources and Acknowledgements

Details for the biographical notes were taken mainly from the following sources:

Who Was Who – *Volume I, 1897–1916*; *Chambers' Scottish Biographical Dictionary*; *Dictionary of National Biography*; *The Provincial Medical Dictionary*; *Encyclopaedia Britannica*; *Hutchinsons Encyclopaedia*; *John Buchan, A Biographical Sketch* by Sheila Scott; *The Gladstones, A Family Biography* by S G Checkland.

Thanks also to the National Library of Scotland and to Brian Lambie of the Biggar Museum Trust for their help in collecting the information.

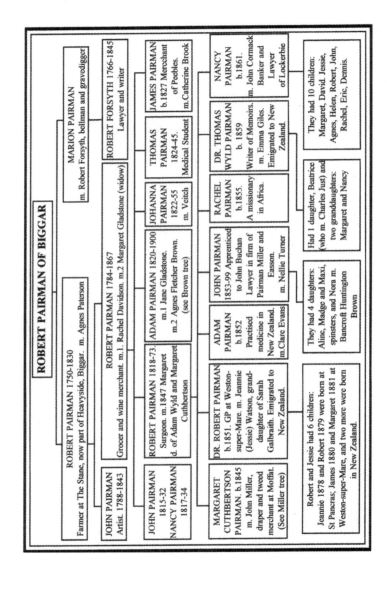

## ROBERT PAIRMAN OF BIGGAR

**ROBERT PAIRMAN 1750-1830**
Farmer at The Stane, now part of Heavyside, Biggar. m. Agnes Paterson

**MARION PAIRMAN**
m. Robert Forsyth, bellman and gravedigger

**ROBERT PAIRMAN 1784-1867**
Grocer and wine merchant. m.1. Rachel Davidson. m.2 Margaret Gladstone (widow)

**ROBERT FORSYTH 1766-1845**
Lawyer and writer

**JOHN PAIRMAN 1788-1843**

**JOHN PAIRMAN 1815-32**
Artist. **NANCY PAIRMAN 1817-34**

**ROBERT PAIRMAN 1818-73.**
Surgeon. m.1847 Margaret d. of Adam Wyld and Margaret Cuthbertson

**ADAM PAIRMAN 1820-1900**
m.1 Jane Gladstone. m.2 Agnes Fletcher Brown. (see Brown tree)

**JOHANNA PAIRMAN 1822-55**
m. Veitch

**THOMAS PAIRMAN 1824-45.**
Medical Student

**JAMES PAIRMAN b.1827** Merchant of Peebles. m.Catherine Brook

**MARGARET CUTHBERTSON PAIRMAN. b.1845**
m. John Miller, draper and tweed merchant at Moffat. (See Miller tree)

**DR. ROBERT PAIRMAN b.1851.** GP at Weston-super-Mare. m. Jeannie (Jessie) Watson, granddaughter of Sarah Galbraith. Emigrated to New Zealand.

**ADAM PAIRMAN b.1852**
Practised medicine in New Zealand. m.Clare Evans

**JOHN PAIRMAN 1853-99** Apprenticed to John Buchan Lawyer in firm of Pairman Miller and Easson. m. Nellie Turner

**RACHEL PAIRMAN b.1855.**
A missionary in Africa.

**DR. THOMAS WYLD PAIRMAN b. 1859**
Writer of Memoirs. m. Emma Giles. Emigrated to New Zealand.

**NANCY PAIRMAN b.1861.**
m. John Cormack Banker and Lawyer of Lockerbie

Robert and Jessie had 6 children:
Jeannie 1878 and Robert 1879 were born at St Pancras; James 1880 and Margaret 1881 at Weston-super-Mare, and two more were born in New Zealand.

They had 4 daughters:
Aline, Madge and Maxi, spinsters, and Nora m. Bancroft Huntington Brown

Had 1 daughter, Beatrice (who m. Charles Just) and two granddaughters: Margaret and Nancy

They had 10 children:
Margaret, David. Jessie, Agnes, Helen, Robert, John, Rachel, Eric, Dennis.

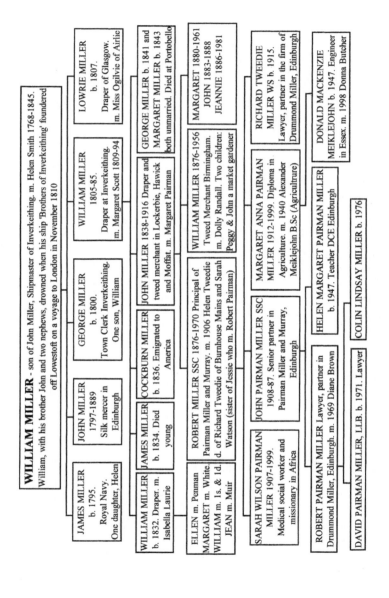

**WILLIAM MILLER** - son of John Miller, Shipmaster of Inverkeithing. m. Helen Smith 1768-1845. William, with his brother John and two nephews, drowned when his ship 'Brothers of Inverkeithing' foundered off Lowestoft on a voyage to London in November 1810

JAMES MILLER b. 1795. Royal Navy. One daughter, Helen

JOHN MILLER 1797-1889 Silk mercer in Edinburgh

GEORGE MILLER b. 1800. Town Clerk Inverkeithing. One son, William

WILLIAM MILLER 1805-85. Draper at Inverkeithing. m. Margaret Scott 1809-94

LOWRIE MILLER b. 1807. Draper of Glasgow. m. Miss Ogilvie of Airlie

WILLIAM MILLER b. 1832. Draper. m. Isabella Laurie

JAMES MILLER b. 1834. Died young

COCKBURN MILLER b. 1836. Emigrated to America

JOHN MILLER 1838-1916 Draper and tweed merchant in Lockerbie, Hawick and Moffat. m. Margaret Pairman

GEORGE MILLER b. 1841 and MARGARET MILLER b. 1843 both unmarried. Died at Portobello

ELLEN m. Penman
MARGARET m. White.
WILLIAM m. 1s. & 1d.
JEAN m. Muir

ROBERT MILLER SSC 1876-1970 Principal of Pairman Miller and Murray. m. 1906 Helen Tweedie d. of Richard Tweedie of Burnhouse Mains and Sarah Watson (sister of Jessie who m. Robert Pairman)

WILLIAM MILLER 1876-1956 Tweed Merchant Birmingham. m. Dolly Randall. Two children: Peggy & John a market gardener

MARGARET 1880-1961
JOHN 1883-1888
JEANNIE 1886-1981

SARAH WILSON PAIRMAN MILLER 1907-1999. Medical social worker and missionary in Africa

JOHN PAIRMAN MILLER SSC 1908-87. Senior partner in Pairman Miller and Murray, Edinburgh

MARGARET ANNA PAIRMAN MILLER 1912-1999. Diploma in Agriculture. m. 1940 Alexander Meiklejohn B.Sc (Agricultrure)

RICHARD TWEEDIE MILLER WS b. 1915. Lawyer, partner in the firm of Drummond Miller, Edinburgh

ROBERT PAIRMAN MILLER Lawyer, partner in Drummond Miller, Edinburgh. m. 1969 Diane Brown

HELEN MARGARET PAIRMAN MILLER b. 1947. Teacher DCE Edinburgh

DONALD MACKENZIE MEIKLEJOHN b. 1947. Engineer in Essex. m. 1998 Donna Butcher

DAVID PAIRMAN MILLER, LLB. b. 1971. Lawyer

COLIN LINDSAY MILLER b. 1976

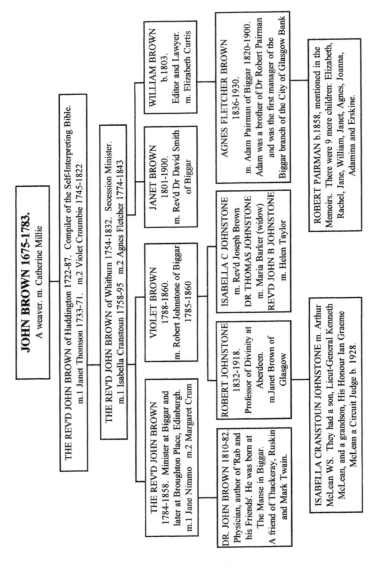

**JOHN BROWN 1675-1783.**
A weaver. m. Catherine Millie

THE REVD JOHN BROWN of Haddington 1722-87. Compiler of the Self-Interpreting Bible.
m.1 Janet Thomson 1733-71. m.2 Violet Croumbie 1745-1822

THE REVD JOHN BROWN of Whitburn 1754-1832. Secession Minister.
m.1 Isabella Cranstoun 1758-95 m.2 Agnes Fletcher 1774-1843

WILLIAM BROWN
b.1803.
Editor and Lawyer.
m. Elizabeth Curtis

JANET BROWN
1801-1900.
m. Revd Dr David Smith
of Biggar

AGNES FLETCHER BROWN
1836-1930.
m. Adam Pairman of Biggar 1820-1900.
Adam was a brother of Dr Robert Pairman
and was the first manager of the
Biggar branch of the City of Glasgow Bank

ROBERT PAIRMAN b.1858, mentioned in the
Memoirs. There were 9 more children: Elizabeth,
Rachel, Jane, William, Janet, Agnes, Joanna,
Adamina and Erskine.

VIOLET BROWN
1788-1860.
m. Robert Johnstone of Biggar
1785-1860

ISABELLA C JOHNSTONE
m. Revd Joseph Brown
DR THOMAS JOHNSTONE
m. Maria Barker (widow)
REVD JOHN B JOHNSTONE
m. Helen Taylor

THE REVD JOHN BROWN
1784-1858. Minister at Biggar and
later at Broughton Place, Edinburgh.
m.1 Jane Nimmo m.2 Margaret Crum

ROBERT JOHNSTONE
1832-1918.
Professor of Divinity at
Aberdeen.
m.Janet Brown of
Glasgow

DR. JOHN BROWN 1810-82.
Physician, author of 'Rab and
his Friends'. He was born at
The Manse in Biggar.
A friend of Thackeray, Ruskin
and Mark Twain.

ISABELLA CRANSTOUN JOHNSTONE m. Arthur
McLean WS. They had a son, Lieut-General Kenneth
McLean, and a grandson, His Honour Ian Graeme
McLean a Circuit Judge b. 1928.

# INDEX

# Index

# Index